The Accidental

Health Sciences
Librarian

Lisa A. Ennis and Nicole Mitchell

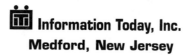 Information Today, Inc.
Medford, New Jersey

First Printing, 2010

The Accidental Health Sciences Librarian

Copyright © 2010 by Lisa A. Ennis and Nicole Mitchell

Library of Congress Cataloging-in-Publication Data

Ennis, Lisa A., 1969-
   The accidental health sciences librarian / Lisa A. Ennis and Nicole Mitchell.
       p. cm.
   Includes bibliographical references and index.
   ISBN 978-1-57387-395-6
   1. Medical Librarianship--United States. 2. Medical Libraries--United States. 3. Library surveys--United States. I. Mitchell, Nicole. II. Title.
   Z675.M4E56 2010
   026'.610973--dc22

                                                                2009051594

Printed and bound in the United States of America

President and CEO: Thomas H. Hogan, Sr.
Editor-in-Chief and Publisher: John B. Bryans
Managing Editor: Amy M. Reeve
Project Editor: Rachel Singer Gordon
VP Graphics and Production: M. Heide Dengler
Book Designer: Kara Mia Jalkowski
Cover Designer: Ashlee Caruolo

www.infotoday.com

Contents

Foreword

I clearly remember the day I chose my career. During high school, I went to a nearby college library to research careers and came home with the idea of becoming a health sciences librarian. My mother and sister helped guide me in this direction: My mother loved working in an academic library, and my sister enjoyed her career as a pharmacist. I wanted to blend the two concepts—libraries and healthcare—and also have a career that allowed me to learn on a daily basis. Further, I wanted a job that provided a lot of variety and was not too specific, as I knew that I would soon become bored without such options.

More than 30 years later, I have no regrets about my decision and can honestly say that I have never experienced the same day twice. I have worked in all kinds of settings (academic medical centers, community hospitals, regional medical libraries), in different parts of the country, and with all kinds of library users. All of this makes for an extremely challenging, yet rewarding, career! Had I had a book like *The Accidental Health Sciences Librarian*, my career choice would have been so much easier, and I would have had a much better clue of what I was getting into by pursuing this path.

The authors of *The Accidental Health Sciences Librarian* are to be congratulated for presenting not just a terrific overview of the field and the infrastructure that supports it (such as the National Library of Medicine), but also for their inclusion of others' stories and journeys. This ensured that they not only expressed their own voices but, through a peer survey and personal testimonies, that they shared others' personal experiences of what makes health sciences librarianship such a valuable and fun profession.

This book encapsulates within its covers numerous personal reflections that provide valuable guidance to those considering a career in health sciences librarianship. With just over 4,000 health sciences librarians in the U.S., our profession is unknown to many—except to those lucky enough (as I was) to know someone in the library field or to have the resources at hand to explore this exciting profession. This book enables a quick discovery of the profession and is a very readable overview of a day in the life of a health sciences librarian.

As the book indicates, health sciences libraries and librarians are unique even within this subfield. Health sciences librarians directly engage with the healthcare enterprise of which the library is a part, and many librarians now, through the wonders of technology, are able to physically be located within healthcare environments rather than library buildings. They can do rounds with healthcare teams (clinical medical librarians), provide synthesized information at the point of need through their additional clinical and research subject knowledge (informationists), and train healthcare providers in using the knowledge and evidence available through years of organizing the medical literature (see Chapter 3). They are vital members of healthcare teams that are examining how to embed such knowledge within electronic medical and personal health records and within the clinical context. They are supporting their institutions by helping to translate research into clinical practice at accelerated speeds, and they are instructors and members of educational curricular committees to ensure that the latest information is applied to the teaching of healthcare students.

The Accidental Health Sciences Librarian is a must-read for all those interested in a profession that will enable them to grow and be rewarded by serving others in the process, as it is "all about the people." It should be promoted by library school educators and become part of library school students' required reading. This book is highly recommended for inclusion in K–12 guidance counseling collections and for those who help to direct students with their career selections.

Jean P. Shipman
Director
Spencer S. Eccles Health Sciences Library
University of Utah
Medical Library Association President 2006–07

Acknowledgments

We would like to thank all the librarians who took time out of their busy schedules to contribute sidebars to this book. We'd also like to thank all the folks who took time to fill out the survey. Thanks also go to our publisher, Information Today, Inc., and our editor, Rachel Singer Gordon.

About the Website

ahslbook.wordpress.com

This book is intended as a starting point for accidental health sciences librarians. As such, it includes numerous websites, resources, and tutorials for learning more about health sciences librarianship. All of these links, as well as additional resources, are available on the book's companion website at ahslbook.word press.com. The authors encourage comments, feedback, and contributions at ahslbook@gmail.com.

Disclaimer

Introduction

I find that a great part of the information I have was acquired by looking something up and finding something else on the way. —Franklin P. Adams

Any librarian, anywhere, may now be asked a health sciences question. Even when channel-surfing on TV, you are bombarded with medical- and health-related shows, from *Mystery Diagnosis* to tips on cooking healthier foods. People are being encouraged to take charge of their health, question their doctors, and live better. Librarians are being asked to do everything from helping a middle school student write a report on the importance of fiber in a healthy diet to helping someone find information on a terminal disease. If you've picked up this book, most likely you've inadvertently found yourself working as a health sciences librarian or have found yourself getting more and more health sciences questions. If so, you've come to the right place.

The Accidental Health Sciences Librarian provides a starting point for accidental health sciences librarians in all library environments, from solo hospital librarians to librarians working for large federal departments. This isn't intended to be a comprehensive textbook (there are plenty of those) or a step-by-step manual (there are plenty of "how-to" books already). Instead, we want to impart a broad overview of the field—and give you a guide written in a casual, easy-to-read style. Since health sciences librarians come from such varied backgrounds, we've intentionally kept the content broad, aiming to hit on the topics common among most health sciences librarians. While we did draw on our own experiences, the content is largely driven by the results we received from the Accidental Health Sciences Librarian Survey (see Appendix A).

In early 2008, we conducted an informal survey using SurveyMonkey (survey questions are reproduced in Appendix A). The survey announcement and link were sent to a variety of lists, and more than 300 librarians responded. Survey results and quotes are included throughout the book—but keep in mind that this was an informal survey. Respondents were overwhelmingly academic or hospital librarians and over 50 years old. In fact, of the 342 librarians who listed their age, 191 (55.8 percent) reported their age as 50 or older. Seventy respondents reported their age as 40–49 years, and 65 reported 30–39, while only 16 librarians were in the 20–29 range. In many cases, the survey raised more questions than it answered, but the results are interesting and definitely provide directions for future research.

We asked people to describe their path to health sciences librarianship in an effort to see how many got into the field accidentally. In all, 336 people responded to the question. While a few knew they wanted to be health sciences librarians, the vast majority ended up in a health sciences library by accident. Typical comments include (identifying information has been removed):

- "Accidental! I was a patient at [a hospital] and walked past the library—popped in to ask if there were any jobs—the rest is history!"

- "My first professional job was part-time reference at [a university]. The local hospital needed a part-time librarian, and a colleague suggested my name, since the previous part-time ref librarian had been the librarian at the hospital as well."

- "Accidental—I had planned to be a general academic librarian but got a part-time job at a med school library while I was a library student and decided I really liked medical librarianship."

- "I was an elementary school librarian for 8 years and wanted a change. This position opened up and I applied."

- "Truly accidental! After 15 years in corporate/special libraries, I was looking for a job after being laid off for the second time. The previous director at this consumer health library was leaving, and I knew her through SLA, contacted her, sent in my resume with her recommendation, and the rest is history. I love it!"

- "Planned to be an archivist or work in a museum, but after grad school, I did an internship with the U.S. Olympic Committee. This introduced me to working in a smaller library as well as the health sciences. My first 'real' job was as an ILL Librarian for a regional public library system. Great first job, but there was no place to move up. The hospital job in town opened up, I applied, and got it. Almost 14 years later, here I am, loving it more than ever."

- "Accidental in the truest sense of the word. I was hired for humanities and someone quit—now I teach EBM (evidence-based medicine) for the medical school."

- "I went to library school to be a children's librarian but graduated right after 9/11, so there were not a lot of jobs available. I applied for this medical librarian job just to continue to get interviewing experience, had *no* expectations on getting the job!"

- "While working in a public library, my scuba diving buddy was chief of surgery at the hospital, and she recommended that I take the position when it opened up."

- "Public librarian for 1.5 years, moved to new state, worked at big university library in variety of positions while searching for 'real' job, found medical library job and took it, even with two other public library job offers on the table, to give it a try."

- "My mom found an article about a hospital librarian and gave it to me and said 'this sounds like something you'd like.'"

- "Rare book room to public library to medical libraries. Someone recommended me for my first medical library job."

- "Accidental: After a few false starts in other careers ... I decided to pursue a master's degree in library science on the recommendation of friends. ... When I asked about tuition assistance, I was offered a traineeship with the Veterans Administration. I never looked back."

If your story sounds similar to these, this book will provide you with advice, information, and resources to help you get your "sea legs" as you navigate the waters of health sciences librarianship. If you are considering health sciences librarianship as a career, you'll get a good glimpse of the broad and varied opportunities that await you if you choose this path. Since both of us were ourselves accidental health sciences librarians, we understand how daunting it can be—and we wrote the book we wished we had had when we started out.

The Accidental Health Sciences Librarian is organized into six chapters. Chapters 1 and 2 provide a broad look at the different kinds of libraries and environments where health sciences librarians can be found and at some of the things, like MeSH, that make health sciences librarianship different from other flavors of librarianship. Chapter 3 deals with the types of patrons you may see and the types of health sciences activities in which you're likely to be involved. Chapter 4 deals with technology, and Chapter 5 covers some of the best-known health sciences resources. Finally, Chapter 6 deals with networking and other resources from which you can find help. We hope this book will be helpful, and we welcome comments and suggestions. Please feel free to contact us at ahslbook@gmail.com.

Chapter 1

Health Sciences Librarianship

The dissemination of knowledge is one of the cornerstones of civilization.
—John F. Budd

People tend to hold two common misconceptions about health sciences librarianship. One is that, to be a health sciences librarian, you must have a science background. The other is that health sciences librarians only work for medical schools or in hospitals. Both of these statements couldn't be further from the truth. Health sciences librarians come from a variety of backgrounds and hold a variety of degrees across the academic spectrum. They also work in a whole host of different settings, including public libraries, academic and community college libraries (as liaison specialists), corporate libraries, federal agencies, and more. Further, health sciences librarians do all the things other librarians do, such as marketing, outreach, instruction, and technical services activities. So while you may focus on a particular subject area in the health sciences, the *librarian* part of health sciences librarianship is as wide open as any other facet of librarianship.

In the Accidental Health Sciences Librarian survey, we asked "In what type of library do you work? Academic, Hospital, Public, AHEC, or Other (please specify)." A total of 344 people responded to this question, and the overwhelming majority (282, or 82 percent) classified themselves as an academic or hospital librarian. Five public librarians and eight Area Health Education Centers

(AHEC) librarians responded as well, leaving 49 people (14 percent) who responded "other." Among those replying "other," we received a variety of responses that show how varied health sciences librarians' roles are; other institutions included association libraries, a community college library, a nursing library, a professional regulatory organization, a state psychiatric center, a nonprofit gerontology research institute, and a nonprofit insurance organization, as well as one institution employing a librarian to do pharmaceutical research and development. So while academic and hospital librarians were most prevalent, the results do demonstrate the numerous different types of organizations in which health sciences librarians may be employed.

As one illustration of this, let's take a look at the Knoxville Area Health Sciences Library Consortium (gsm.utmck.edu/library/kahslc/kahslc.htm). This 15-member organization's mission is "to promote better communication, sharing of resources, and continuing education among health sciences librarians in the Knoxville area." This one consortium includes the Knoxville Public Library, two community colleges, the National Limb Loss Information Center, the Pediatric Library of the East Tennessee Children's Hospital, and the Oak Ridge National Laboratory Research Libraries—as well as a variety of academic libraries.

If you find yourself in a health sciences setting, consider yourself lucky. You have the unique opportunity to get real experience in an area that many consider too specialized or too difficult to tackle. Once you have that experience, it is worth its weight in gold, whether you decide to stay in the field, move into a different facet of health sciences librarianship, or even move into some other sort of librarianship. If you want to break into the health sciences, the best way to begin is by grabbing every available opportunity to play in the sciences. Volunteer for science liaison areas, join a relevant association, develop research interests in the health sciences, and present papers and publish on health sciences topics. Believe us when we say that a willingness to tackle health sciences in any way you can will not go unnoticed.

Help! My Degree Is in English

On the survey we also asked "What other degrees do you hold? Please list all degrees, fields, and schools." The responses reflected a wide range of disciplines, ranging from home economics to folklore. We tallied all the responses that included a bachelor's degree (300) to determine the most common undergraduate majors among the survey respondents. Here are the results:

- English: 44
- History: 30
- Education: 25
- Biology: 18
- Anthropology: 14
- Psychology: 12
- Business: 8
- Library science: 8
- Nursing: 8

Of the 300 respondents who listed their bachelor's degrees, 15 percent held undergraduate degrees in English, and 25 percent held a degree in either history or English. Whatever your undergraduate degree is in, don't let it hinder you from becoming a health sciences librarian.

Both of us have a bachelor's and a master's in history (see our paths to health sciences librarianship in "About the Authors" at the end of this book). True, a degree in the sciences will be noted in the plus column when you apply for jobs—but, just as when applying for any library job, multiple factors determine whether you get the job offer. Further, if you do accidentally find yourself in a health sciences position with a degree in English or in history (or in anything else, for that matter), don't feel that this is a hurdle to be overcome. Whatever your background, you bring a unique skill set and personality to the job—so use both to your advantage.

On the survey we also asked if people took a health sciences course in library school. If the answer was no, we asked whether it was because their program didn't offer one, whether they chose not to, or whether the course didn't fit their schedule. We also provided a space for people to respond with "other" reasons. Of the 344 respondents, 146 (42.4 percent) reported that they did take a health sciences course in library school, while 198 (57.6 percent) said they did not. Of those who responded that they didn't take a health sciences class, 92 (46.5 percent) said that no course was offered at their school, 44 (22.2 percent) said they chose not to take the class, 25 (12.6 percent) reported that the course didn't fit their schedule, and 37 (18.7 percent) reported some other reason for not taking a health sciences class. So while a library school course in health sciences would certainly be useful, don't let your lack of one stop you from applying for a health sciences job.

Don't All Health Sciences Librarians Work in a Hospital or Medical School Library?

Don't make the mistake of thinking that health sciences librarians only work in libraries attached to a hospital or medical school. Just as health sciences librarians have varied backgrounds, they can also be found in a wide range of settings—and even hospital and academic libraries vary widely. The following sections provide a sampling of some of the settings in which you might find health sciences librarians. While this list is far from exhaustive, it should give you a sense of how diverse the field of health sciences librarianship really is.

Academic Libraries

While libraries attached to medical schools are definitely academic, a host of other academic health sciences libraries serve all sorts of clienteles. For instance, the Lister Hill Library of the Health Sciences at the University of Birmingham (www.uab.edu/lister) does serve the School of Medicine, but it also serves six other professional schools, the campus, and a hospital, and includes a very well-known historical collection. The four-story library has a staff of more than 40; its atmosphere is very much like that of any large academic library. Another example of a large health sciences library attached to a university is the University of New Mexico Health Sciences Library and Informatics Center (hsc.unm.edu/library).

On the other hand, the Maguire Medical Library at the Florida State University College of Medicine (www.med.fsu.edu/library) can be found in one large room housed within the College of Medicine building and only has a staff of about five. However, Maguire still serves six regional medical campuses and two rural training locations in Florida. Sometimes, regional campuses will also have their own library. For instance, the Huntsville Regional Medical Campus is part of the University of Alabama School of Medicine, and it houses the Sparks Medical Library (main.uab.edu/uasom/2/show.asp?durki=20025). The Sparks Library has a staff of two and serves mainly third- and fourth-year medical students and residents. Each medical library, large or small, is designed and staffed to serve the particular needs of its campus. You can find academic health sciences libraries of any size, so you have the option of a number of different work environments.

One main difference between academic health sciences libraries and medical school libraries is that, in a health sciences library that serves a larger academic community, you'll have the opportunity to work with a wider variety of students, clinicians, and medical professionals. For instance, we are liaisons to the School of Optometry and the School of Nursing, respectively. We rarely interact with the medical school, but we do encounter students from all over campus—including an occasional English literature student. By contrast, the Greenblatt Library at the Medical College of Georgia (www.lib.mcg.edu) is strictly a health sciences campus with five professional schools, including graduate programs in medical dosimetry (the measurement and calculation of dosage for the treatment of cancer patients) and medical illustration. You can begin to see just from these few examples how different these health sciences libraries can be, even though they are all called *academic* health sciences libraries.

The vast majority of academic health sciences libraries have their own director and report directly to a university provost or dean (or the dean of or director within the medical school), while a few report to another library director on campus. This can give a health sciences library a good bit of autonomy and the ability to set its own goals and priorities, as its money comes from a separate pot rather than having to be carved out of another library's budget. When interviewing for academic health sciences librarian positions, be sure you know how the library's administration is set up. Ask questions that can give you hints as to how the libraries on a campus interact with each other—especially if your potential boss reports to a director in another library.

Many general academic libraries serve health sciences schools as well. For instance, many community colleges, liberal arts colleges, and universities have nursing, allied health, and other health sciences programs. Keene State College's Mason Library (www.keene.edu/library) in New Hampshire supports programs in health sciences, physical education, and athletic training, while the University of North Carolina at Asheville Ramsey Library (www.lib.unca.edu/library) has a liaison for health and wellness.

Libraries such as Georgia State University Library (www.library. gsu.edu) in Atlanta serve health programs such as the College of Health and Human Sciences, which includes the School of Nursing, Division of Nutrition, Institute of Public Health, and the Center for Healthy Development.

Some health-oriented academic institutions also have stand-alone libraries. For example, the Galen College of Nursing (www. galened.com), the New York University College of Dentistry (www. nyu.edu/dental), and the New England College of Optometry (www.neco.edu) all have their own libraries. Chiropractic schools, such as the Palmer College of Chiropractic, also maintain libraries. The David D. Palmer Health Sciences Library (www.palmer.edu/ libraryd.aspx), named for the founder of modern chiropractic, contains special collections and archives considered the "most comprehensive chiropractic historical resource in the world."[1] So health sciences librarians can find themselves in all sorts of academic settings, from small community colleges to huge research universities with hospitals and clinics. If you end up in an academic health sciences library, the key is not to get so overwhelmed by all the health sciences stuff that you ignore the importance of learning about the work environment.

Typical day-to-day tasks for an academic health sciences librarian depend largely on the type and size of the library. Large academic health sciences libraries employ all sorts of librarians, from behind-the-scenes types like systems librarians and catalogers to the reference and instruction people on the front lines. In smaller libraries, most technical services functions may be handled by the main library on campus. For instance, the health sciences staff might develop the library's collection but send lists of purchases to the main library, whose acquisitions people will do the actual ordering and whose catalogers will enter the books into a shared catalog.

In any academic setting, be sure you understand the faculty issues and requirements that go along with your job. For instance, at Lister Hill we have faculty rank and status but do not have tenure. At Maguire, librarians have faculty status and faculty rank, but no tenure. This all depends on the library and the institution, so just know what you are getting into when you accept the job. You don't want promotion or tenure sneaking up on you! Get a handle on what is required as soon as you can, so that you can start squirreling away documentation and make sure to do everything you need to do to get promoted or be granted tenure. Also ask if any librarians at your institution have appointments in the medical or other schools. In some cases, librarians have become such an integral part of a school that they hold faculty status within that school.

Along these lines, also be sure you understand the service component of your job. Most academic libraries will require some form of professional service. This can include activities such as serving on local, state, or national library association committees or groups, as well as on various committees within the library and/or college. Another component to be aware of is the scholarship requirements of your position. Academic library jobs also require some sort of scholarship, whether this be writing book reviews or articles, presenting posters or papers at a conference, or serving as an editor. It may seem overwhelming at first, but you'll soon settle into a groove.

Veterinary Libraries

Veterinary libraries are another flavor of health sciences libraries. These libraries are often, but not always, attached to a university and sometimes also will be responsible for serving a school's agricultural programs (and hence are sometimes referred to as Ag/Vet libraries). The Veterinary Medical Libraries Section (VMLS; www.vmls.mlanet. org) of the Medical Library Association (MLA) is a great place to learn about this facet of health sciences librarianship. VMLS also maintains a veterinary libraries directory that lists veterinary libraries world-wide (www.vmls.mlanet.org/vlindex.htm), and its diversity shows that even this one subspecialty has enough variety to keep anyone interested and challenged.

The title of this book is a perfect way to explain my being a veterinary medical librarian. With fewer than 30 veterinary medical schools in the U.S., there are not many opportunities in this field of librarianship. In addition to working at academic institutions, veterinary medical librarians can be found at zoos and wild animal parks, aquariums, veterinary associations, and animal research centers.

The combination of education, experience, luck, and being in the right place at the right time all came together for me. While my formal education and degrees are in the social sciences, I worked as a para-professional in an engineering branch library at a large research university. This influenced my desire to learn more and to obtain my master's degree in library science and take science reference courses.

Thirty years later, I've worked at both academic and public libraries. For the majority of that time, I held management positions, supervising librarians, staff, student workers, and volunteers. Given my strong background of experience in the sciences and management, combined with a commitment to user services, when an opening at my institution for the head of a veterinary branch library became available, I leaped at the opportunity to apply. I have now been a veterinary medical librarian since 2003.

A good job allows for a variety of duties, opportunities, growth, and challenges. Within a couple of weeks of starting my new position, I was asked to draw a floor plan to renovate the existing library. Definitely challenging—but also rewarding when you see it all come to fruition. Redesigning a library is not an everyday event, but working with a broad range of library users is. Veterinary librarians serve not only the individuals currently affiliated with their institution but also alums, veterinary practitioners, and animal owners. And, as often found in other areas of medical librarianship, you're often called upon during an emergency or crisis—which can be a life-or-death situation.

Pet owners often visit the library while they wait for a test or other procedures to be performed on their pet, so the importance of a sympathetic, caring library staff cannot be overemphasized. And it's not unusual for one of the surgeons or clinicians to seek us out for information needed in a very short time frame. Because I work at an academic institution with a college of veterinary medicine, I work with DVM [Doctor of Veterinary Medicine] students starting from their first day of library orientation during their first week on campus until their graduation four years later. It's very rewarding to work with the students, from assisting them with their basic introductory courses to helping them with the information they need for their rotations.

The rewards are many in this career. Knowing that the information found through library resources can save someone's pet or that the research done contributes to the overall wellness of humans, as in cancer research, is very satisfying. With their understanding of disease models, veterinarians also play a vital role in public health. It's the veterinary librarian's role to make sure that practitioners have the right tools at their disposal. The best perk of the job is the veterinarians and DVM students! They're always pleasant to work with, they're quick to say "thank you," and they love and use their libraries.

Cindy Mitchell is the Veterinary Medicine and Biomedical Sciences Librarian at Colorado State University Libraries (lib.colostate.edu) in Fort Collins, Colorado.

For instance, you might find yourself working at a library like the University of Tennessee at Knoxville's Pendergrass Agriculture & Veterinary Medicine Library (www.lib.utk.edu/agvet). The Pendergrass Library has a staff of about six and "holds the majority of the University Libraries' collections for agriculture, natural and environmental sciences, food sciences, and veterinary medicine."[2] You might, on the other hand, find yourself working at a library such as the University of Georgia's Science Library (www.libs.uga.edu/science). Here, you'll find a "broad range of materials in agriculture, biological and life sciences, human and veterinary medicine, mathematics, computer science, physical sciences, engineering and technology" and a staff of more than 20 that also supports the university's College of Veterinary Medicine, Agricultural Experiment Stations, Skidaway Institute of Oceanography, Sapelo Island Marine Institute, and Veterinary Diagnostic Laboratory.[3] Veterinary libraries can narrow their focus even more. For example, the Gluck Equine Research Center Library at the University of Kentucky (www.ca.uky.edu/gluck/ServLibrary.asp) deals with everything about horses, while the Oregon Health & Science University maintains the Isabel McDonald Library at the Oregon National Primate Research Center (www.ohsu.edu/library/primate.shtml)—which, of course, focuses on primates.

An academic veterinary library is generally classified as a branch library falling under the directorship of the main library on campus. This usually means that most technical services activities happen in the main library, leaving the veterinary library staff free to focus on such things as collection development, reference, research, and instruction. Again, as with any academic position, make sure you learn the ins and outs of faculty status, tenure, and what is required for promotion.

Not all veterinary libraries are attached to schools. For instance, the Zoological Society of San Diego runs the society's library (library.sandiegozoo.org), located within the famed San Diego Zoo (seriously, how cool is that?!), while the Baltimore Aquarium houses the A. Carter Middendorf Library (www.aqua.org). For a complete list of zoo and aquarium libraries, see the Directory of Zoo and Aquarium Libraries at www.nal.usda.gov/awic/zoo/Zoo AquaLibDir.htm. Another interesting veterinary library is the Smithsonian's National Zoological Park (NZP) Branch Library (www.sil.si.edu/libraries/nzp). One of 20 libraries that make up the Smithsonian Institution Libraries system, the NZP Branch Library houses a monograph and serial collection as well as a special collection "of publications from other zoos and aquariums such as animal collection inventories, annual reports, guidebooks and miscellaneous pamphlets," some of which are more than 100 years old.[4] The federal government also runs its share of animal-related libraries, such as the U.S. Department of Agriculture's National Agricultural Library (NAL; www.nal.usda.gov) and smaller entities that fall under the NAL, such as the Animal Welfare Information Center (awic.nal.usda.gov).

If these examples pique your interest in Ag/Vet libraries, don't be afraid to contact an Ag/Vet librarian and ask about the job. You can browse the list on the VMLS website for contact information and to find Ag/Vet libraries in your area. If you are still in library school, and your university also has a veterinary school, ask about doing an internship or practicum. Doing an internship is the best way to find out if you'll like something and to learn about the day-to-day routine.

Area Health Education Centers

Developed by Congress in 1971, the Area Health Education Centers, or AHEC, program is charged with recruiting, training, and retaining a "health professions workforce committed to underserved populations" by harnessing the resources of academic medicine. There are currently 54 AHEC programs operating more than 200 centers,[5] and the National AHEC Organization (NAO) maintains a directory of AHEC programs at www.national ahec.org/Directory/AHECDirectory.asp. By browsing the directory you can see that there is a good deal of variation among these programs. Some don't employ librarians, but a number of them do.

Just a few examples show how each AHEC can be set up differently. The University of Arkansas for Medical Sciences' AHEC program, founded in 1973, highlights its library services: "AHEC Learning Resource Centers supply library resources to programs, institutions, and individuals throughout Arkansas, serving as regional medical and health professional information specialists."[6] These consist of seven different libraries around the state (www.uams.edu/AHEC/library.asp). Directed by a librarian, the Foothills AHEC program (www.foothillsahec.org) is a partnership between local communities and educators in northeast Georgia, while the North Carolina AHEC Information and Library System (library.ncahec.net/ILS) divides the state into nine regions, each with its own AHEC that includes "library and information services to support the clinical, educational, and research activities of regional health professionals and students."[7] North Carolina also provides the AHEC Digital Library (ADL; library.ncahec.net). Both institutions and individuals can purchase a membership to the ADL; an individual membership is $150 per year as of 2009.[8]

AHECs vary widely, as they are born out of the specific needs of a geographical area—and may or may not include librarians on their teams. Requirements in the job ads for AHEC librarians similarly vary, but outreach, reference, and instruction are generally important components. One typical ad, for instance, states that the "librarian's primary responsibility is the administration of an … outreach project providing library services and training to public health professionals in the region." The introduction to the North Florida AHEC (www.northfloridaahec.org) sums it up nicely:

> We're not neurologists.
> But we strengthen minds every day.
> We're not cardiologists.
> But we inspire the hearts of caregivers.
> We're not optometrists.
> But we help the medically underserved see a brighter
>   future.[9]

Hospital Libraries, Veterans Affairs Medical Libraries, and Patient Education Libraries

As with all the other types of libraries we've looked at, libraries attached to hospitals can vary greatly. Most are small in terms of both space and personnel; often they are staffed by a solo librarian who is responsible for the entire operation. Due to space limitations, hospital libraries generally focus on having a lean, mean, core collection of materials and providing electronic access to the most current and relevant resources. This fits in nicely with the needs of their clientele, who tend to be very busy healthcare practitioners and clinicians. They want the most current information, they want it delivered to their computer or handheld device—and they want it now! The scope of a hospital library's collection and services should match the goals and mission of the organization to which it is attached. For instance, a teaching hospital's library will need resources geared toward students as well as practitioners and clinicians.

Along the same lines, the organizational structure of a hospital library's parent institution can pose some interesting challenges for hospital librarians—libraries can literally fall anywhere within the hospital's hierarchy. If you work in a hospital library attached to a university hospital, you may find yourself reporting to two bosses—one in the hospital and one in the parent library. While having a stake in two larger entities may give the library a bit more security, reporting to two bosses gets tricky. It's important to realize that, no matter whom you directly report to, you should work to create a good pool of library advocates from all over the hospital. Be aware and flexible when opportunities arise to make both the library and yourself visible and valuable.

Some things to know: If you find yourself working in a hospital library, you will sooner or later hear about the Joint Commission (www.jointcommission.org), formerly the Joint Commission on Accreditation of Healthcare Organizations. The Joint Commission's mission is "to continuously improve health care for the public, in collaboration with other stakeholders, by evaluating health care organizations and inspiring them to excel in providing safe and effective care of the highest quality and value."[10] Accreditation is voluntary, so make sure you find out whether your hospital is seeking or maintaining accreditation status. In any medical setting, you will also most definitely hear the term *HIPAA* thrown about. HIPAA, which stands for the Health Insurance Portability and Accountability Act, is discussed in depth in Chapter 3. Technology and electronic access issues can also be especially problematic for hospital libraries behind tightly guarded firewalls, so for more on technology, see Chapter 4.

If you are looking for more information on hospital libraries, check out MLA's active Hospital Libraries Section (www.hls. mlanet.org/organization), as well as its wiki (mla-hls.wiki spaces.com). You can also browse the internet for examples of the variety of hospital libraries, but keep in mind that hospital library websites may either be really small or buried within a hospital's larger site. For instance, the St. Luke's Cornwall Hospital website (www.stlukescornwallhospital.org) doesn't even provide a direct link to the library from the hospital's main page; visitors have to select the "Health Links" button, then scroll to the end of the list to see "Medical Library" (www.slchlibrary.org). The El Camino Hospital, however, links to its Health Library and Resource Center (www.elcaminohospital.org/Patient_Services/Health_Library) on its main page under the section titled "About Us." The Health Library and Resource Center is a bit more visible because the hospital is advertising the library as a "free community resource open to the public" as well as serving the healthcare practitioners and clinicians within the hospital.[11] See the next section of this chapter for more on consumer health services librarians.

Health sciences librarians are also found in the U.S. Department of Veterans Affairs (VA) libraries. The American Library Association established the VA Library Service during World War I, and then in 1923 the service was absorbed into the Veterans Bureau, predecessor to the VA. According to the VA Library Network (VALNET; www1.va.gov/valnet), VA libraries "provide knowledge-based information for clinical and management decision-making, research, and education."[12]

Like other hospital libraries, VA libraries may be staffed by just one or two people. Depending on the mission of the main institution, the size and scope of VA libraries vary greatly, as do the activities in which librarians are involved. VA librarians provide services to veterans and their families, as well as clinicians, residents, and students, and perform diverse activities, from attending morning reports or staff meetings to performing database searches and providing education sessions to both patients and medical staff. Many libraries, like the Patient Education Resource Center (www.houston. va.gov/PatientEd/perc.asp) at the Michael E. DeBakey VA Medical Center in Houston, Texas, have placed some information resources online. The VA Long Beach Healthcare System also provides a webpage with library information and a link to its catalog (www.long beach.va.gov/Our_Services/library.asp).

VALNET maintains a list of consumer health resources, including information on health literacy, information therapy, post-traumatic stress disorder, and traumatic brain injuries. Librarians also publish a bibliography of resources on "VA priority areas" such as end-of-life care, chemical and biological terrorism, and pain management. Several documents and example policies are available on the VAL-NET site for VA librarians, so this is a good place to start when looking for information and resources on patient computer use, how to evaluate electronic resources, and how to prove the value of a library.

Medical school students learn the saying, "When you hear hoofbeats, think horses, not zebras." This means that when presented with a set of symptoms, doctors are taught to focus on the most common possibility. Sometimes, though, it *is* a zebra making those hoofbeats. Even though we've continually talked about the variety among hospital libraries, there are some that are zebras. Hospital libraries can be found not just in hospital facilities themselves but in a variety of places, including prisons, military bases, and more. For instance, there are circuit librarians who travel to rural hospitals without individual libraries in order to provide library services such as interlibrary loan, literature searches, and help with technology. Many medical departments, like the Department of Ophthalmology or the Department of Surgery, will have separate departmental libraries. Even under the one umbrella of hospital librarianship, you can find a great deal of variety and opportunity.

Consumer Health Libraries

Consumer health librarians can be found in academic, hospital, or public libraries as well as in consumer health and patient education libraries. As we mentioned in the introduction, though, any librarian who comes in contact with the public has the potential to get consumer health questions. These can range from "What does MRSA stand for?" (the answer is methicillin-resistant *Staphylococcus aureus*) to heart-wrenching questions about a loved one who has just been diagnosed with a terminal illness. Knowing where to find consumer health information and making contact with consumer health librarians can help you immensely when confronted with such questions. Just remember that you can't practice medicine (see Chapter 3 for more information on ethics).

The MLA's Consumer and Patient Health Information Section (CAPHIS; caphis.mlanet.org/consumer) defines consumer health as "an umbrella term encompassing the continuum extending from the specific information needs of patients to the broader provision of health information for the lay person."[13] The National Network of Libraries of Medicine (NN/LM; nnlm.gov) sums up consumer health information nicely:

> Consumer health information is simply health or medical information produced or intended for people who are not health professionals. Consumer health information helps people to understand their health and make health-related decisions for themselves or someone else. It also includes information about prevention and wellness. Consumer health information can be found anywhere from pharmacies, grocery stores, and health food stores, to bookstores, physicians offices, libraries, and of course, the World Wide Web.[14]

In other words, consumer health is about turning "pharmaceutical mechanization" into "how this drug works."

Given today's proliferation of available health information, consumer health and patient information libraries are especially important. Consumer health librarians are active in promoting health literacy and providing health information. In "The Librarian's Role in the Provision of Consumer Health Information and Patient Education," CAPHIS outlines the many tasks in which these types of librarians may be involved. As in any library, these activities include collection management, knowledge and resource sharing, advocacy, access, and dissemination of information, education, and research. Consumer health librarians are also engaged in planning seminars and education programs, sharing resources, partnering with community organizations to establish health information events, speaking on various issues, and more.

Some consumer health examples include the Eskind Biomedical Library at Vanderbilt Medical Center's Consumer Health Digital Library (www.mc.vanderbilt.edu/vumcdiglib/subjres. html?diglib=6). In addition to providing access to consumer health resources such as MedlinePlus, the library links to medical dictionaries, encyclopedias, and evidence-based patient information and provides a consumer health resources news channel. In 1985, the University of Connecticut Health Center established a consumer health program, Healthnet (library.uchc.edu/ departm/hnet/about.html), for Connecticut residents and public libraries. As a "librarian to librarian outreach program," Healthnet librarians provide training to public librarians and consumers on how to locate health information, in addition to other activities such as creating public awareness programs and resource guides for both consumers and librarians.[15] The PlaneTree Health Library (www.planetreesanjose.org) in Los Gatos, California, around since 1989, features a book, journal, and audiovisual collection and an on-site bookstore. The library also sponsors health

So, how does someone with a very limited understanding of human biology—as well as a definite squeamishness around even photos of blood and body parts—end up as a medical/consumer health librarian? Well, serendipity helps, as does having the "confidence of the ignorant" (Orson Welles). I first considered medical librarianship after having been a government documents librarian in the local public library for a few years; when a friend retired from her hospital librarian position, I asked her about the job. She proceeded to tell me all about it, including her degrees in relevant sciences as well as the required MLS. I thought about my own undergraduate career in liberal arts with a major in avoiding biology and chemistry at all costs and decided against applying for my friend's erstwhile position at the hospital.

However, a few years later another hospital librarian friend decided to leave her position when her husband got a job out of state. For some reason, this friend looked at me in my public library reference job and thought I would be the perfect replacement for her. She then recruited me with many idealized portraits of the marvels of clinical librarianship as well as much flattery about my own librarian skills. In no time, I was primed for a major job change. The career path switch wasn't exactly smooth, however. My initial visions of a warm family of dedicated colleagues in my new hospital environment (including handsome, George Clooney-like doctors to flirt with) were soon dispelled by an army of demanding, time-challenged healthcare workers who were none too patient with my feverish attempts to learn to search MEDLINE on the fly.

Furthermore, I soon discovered that the hospital business could be brutal. In my two years at this particular hospital, I went through three vice president bosses, each of whom was laid off or otherwise "relocated" for some obscure administrative reason. (I seriously began to wonder if it were the Mafia rather than the Baptists running the place.) Eventually, however, I found my groove in the job, and it got even better when I moved to an academic medical library at a local university. By taking advantage of whatever CE [continuing education] opportunities were available and through simple environmental exposure, I gradually came to a fair command of medical terminology and the finer points of MEDLINE, as well as several other health and science databases. With the support of my newer, more stable administration at the academic medical library, I started a cooperative consumer health information service with my old colleagues at the public libraries, a service that has since grown to serve the entire state and is an affiliate of the National Library of Medicine's MedlinePlus "Go Local" initiative. I love this work!

Moral of the story? I suppose it's that the "confidence of the ignorant" can truly become the confidence of the competent for even the least likely candidates among us—and I'm living proof of that!

Kay Hogan Smith is Community Services Librarian at Lister Hill Library of the Health Sciences at the University of Alabama at Birmingham (www.uab.edu/lister) in Birmingham, Alabama.

lectures at local libraries and a monthly book club. The New York University (NYU) Health Sciences Libraries maintains three consumer health libraries: the Health & Education Resource Center (www.nyupatientlibrary.org/cancer) for the NYU Cancer Institute, the Patient and Family Resource Center (www.nyupatientlibrary.org/medcenter) for the NYU Langone Medical Center, and the Family Health Resource Center & Patient Library (www.nyu patientlibrary.org/hassenfeld) for the Children's Center for Cancer and Blood Disorders. All of these libraries provide patient handouts, links to reliable health websites, and tips on finding and evaluating online health information.

Learning Resource Centers and Simulation Labs

Other interesting settings where you might find a health sciences librarian include learning resource centers (LRCs) and simulation labs. An LRC may be part of a library or something totally separate; simulation labs may fall under the LRC umbrella but can also be totally separate. For example, Mercer University has the Mercer Medical Library and the Peyton T. Anderson Learning Resources Center (medicine.mercer.edu/library_home). The Mercer website clearly outlines the different services offered by the library and the LRC. Library services include things like literature searches, reference services, reserves, interlibrary loan, and the like, while LRC services focus on providing audiovisual and computer equipment as well as a wet lab.[16]

In addition to the Mayo Clinic's library system, one of the largest in the world, the Mayo Medical School has an LRC (www.mayo.edu/mms/learning-resource-center.html). It defines the LRC as "a library facility that supports the medical school curriculum" and that has "a small, carefully selected collection of current medical textbooks. It also provides audiovisual materials, anatomical models and computer-aided educational programs. Several special collections are available including: women's issues in medicine and health; medical education; examination review books and other selected ethics and humanities materials."[17]

Historical Collections

One of the most fascinating areas of health sciences librarianship is the various health- and medical-related historical collections. The most well-known history of medicine collection, and one of the world's largest, is the National Library of Medicine's History of Medicine collection (www.nlm.nih.gov/hmd). Another example is the David D. Palmer Health Sciences Library of the Palmer College of Chiropractic (mentioned previously as a standalone academic library), which is the most thorough chiropractic historical resource available. Lister Hill Library of the Health Sciences has a historical collections department consisting of the University Archives, the Alabama Museum of the Health Sciences, and the Reynolds Historical Library, which contains more than 13,000 rare books, including 30 incunabula as well as an extensive collection on Civil War medicine (www.uab.edu/reynolds). The Michigan State University Libraries' Special Collections houses one of the largest veterinary medical collections in the world (spc.lib.msu.edu/html/materials/collections/vetmed_coll.jsp). Positions in these libraries will most likely require a second degree in history or another appropriate degree. If you find yourself working in (and enjoying your job at) a health sciences library but are also interested in history, MLA has a History of the Health Sciences section (www.mla-hhss.org) you can join to learn more—and the connections you make may lead to a new job.

Conclusion

The preceding sections provide just a glimpse into the kaleidoscope that is health sciences librarianship. Clearly it is a diverse and dynamic field. But what do other librarians have to say about the profession? On the survey, we asked, "What do you love about being a health sciences librarian?" "What are your *least* favorite things about being in health sciences librarianship?" and "What are the greatest challenges in health sciences librarianship today?" Comments ranged from thoughtful and heartfelt to just plain hysterical. Overall, though, a number of common themes emerged (for a sampling of comments, see Appendix B at the end of this book).

Responses to the question "What do you love about being a health sciences librarian?" overwhelmingly focused on helping people and making a difference in people's lives. Another popular response revolved around having new challenges every day. The question "What are your *least* favorite things about being in health sciences librarianship?" also revealed some overarching themes. Many responses centered around the broad issue of recognition— whether concerning low salaries, having to justify the library, or just a general frustration that people don't know what librarians have to offer. Diminishing budgets and the rising cost of materials and resources were also common themes. The responses to "What are the greatest challenges in health sciences librarianship today?" parallel the responses to the least favorite things about health sciences librarianship. A number of responses involved the survival of libraries as the greatest challenge today, while others focused on technology issues as the greatest challenge. Overall, there were no big surprises in any of the responses, and most were positive about the profession as a whole.

Endnotes

1. "Palmer's Davenport Campus Library Special Services Division," www.palmer.edu/libraryd_content.aspx?id=1386
2. Webster C. Pendergrass Agriculture & Veterinary Medicine Library, "History," www.lib.utk.edu/agvet/@pendergrass/history.html
3. University of Georgia Libraries, "About the Science Library," www.libs.uga.edu/science/aboutsci.html

4. National Zoological Park Library, "About the Library," www.sil.si.edu/libraries/nzp/nzp_about.cfm

5. National AHEC Organization, "About Us," www.nationalahec.org/About/AboutUs.asp

6. University of Arkansas for Medical Sciences, Area Health Education Centers, "Learning Resource Centers," www.uams.edu/ahec/LearningResources.asp

7. North Carolina AHEC Information and Library System, "Find an AHEC Library," library.ncahec.net/ILS/location.cfm

8. AHEC Digital Library, "ADL Membership Information," library.ncahec.net/membership.cfm?s=0

9. North Florida AHEC, "Intro," www.northfloridaahec.org

10. Joint Commission, "Facts about The Joint Commission," www.jointcommission.org/AboutUs/Fact_Sheets/joint_commission_facts.htm

11. El Camino Hospital, "Health Library and Resource Center," www.elcaminohospital.org/Patient_Services/Health_Library

12. U.S. Department of Veteran Affairs, "VA Library Network (VALNET)," www1.va.gov/valnet

13. Consumer and Patient Health Information Section, "Purpose," caphis.mlanet.org/organization/membership.html

14. National Network of Libraries of Medicine, "The Growing Demand for Health Information," nnlm.gov/outreach/community/community.html

15. Lyman Maynard Stowe Library, "Healthnet Program Summary," library.uchc.edu/departm/hnet/about.html

16. Mercer University School of Medicine, "About the Medical Library," medicine.mercer.edu/Library/About%20the%20Library/about

17. Mayo Clinic, Mayo Medical School, "Learning Resource Center," www.mayo.edu/mms/learning-resource-center.html

Chapter 2

Putting the Medical in Health Sciences Librarianship

American citizens, for whom the health of their loved ones is always of primary concern, can take great pride in their National Library of Medicine, which takes life-giving knowledge from research, organizes it, and transmits it to those who can best use it to fight disease and disability and to improve the quality of life for all of us.

—President Ronald Reagan

How much medicine do you really need to know to be an effective health sciences librarian? On your first day, not a whole lot! A willingness to learn and a natural curiosity will provide you with the drive to learn more and more every day. We are amazed at how much we've both learned and grown over the past few years. For instance, one of us (we won't tell you which) once went strolling through the stacks looking for nursing books in the RTs. That's right: Coming from an academic background, the author was looking for the Library of Congress (LC) call number (RT), when instead she should have been looking for the National Library of Medicine (NLM) call number (WY). At least it didn't take her too long to figure out the error.

Whenever you take a new job, whether you've been a librarian for two weeks or 20 years, you have to give yourself time to adjust to the new setting. No two libraries do things the same way, even if they are the same kind of library, but there are some commonalities. This chapter will give you a leg up—and keep you from aimlessly roaming the stacks. You'll get a good overview of the NLM and some of the basic tools used in the health sciences.

National Library of Medicine: A Brief History

The NLM (www.nlm.nih.gov), part of the National Institutes of Health (NIH), has its origins in the Library of the Office of the Surgeon General of the U.S. Army (established in 1836). In 1865, Dr. John Shaw Billings (1838–1913), a field surgeon in the Union army, became the first director for the library—which was then housed at Ford's Theatre after President Abraham Lincoln's assassination there. Dr. Billings formed the library's mission to collect and index the world's medical literature and by 1873 had increased the library's collection from just 1,800 to more than 50,000 items. He served as director until 1895, when he became director of the New York Public Library. At that time, the library's collection encompassed more than 300,000 books and pamphlets.

The Library of the Office of the Surgeon General of the U.S. Army was renamed the Army Medical Library in 1922, and in April 1952 changed into the Armed Forces Medical Library. In 1954, the Hoover Commission Task Force on Federal Medical Services determined that a National Library of Medicine should be established and that it should incorporate the collection from the Armed Forces Medical Library. After the Hoover Commission's report, Senators John F. Kennedy (MA) and Lister Hill (AL) proposed and submitted to Congress the current NLM, created as an amendment to Title III of the Public Health Service Act on March 13, 1956.

President Dwight D. Eisenhower signed the bill into law on August 3, 1956, declaring that the NLM was established "in order to assist the advancement of medical and related sciences and to aid the dissemination and exchange of scientific and other information important to the progress of medicine and to the public health."[1] This amendment transferred the existing Armed Forces Medical Library into the Public Health Service and renamed it the National Library of Medicine on October 1, 1956. The act included provisions for a new facility on the campus of the National Institutes of Health in Bethesda, Maryland; the new NLM building was dedicated in December 1961 and opened to the public in 1962. Today, the NLM is the world's largest medical library, containing more than 9 million items. A detailed history appears in Wyndham D. Miles' *A History of the National Library of Medicine: The Nation's Treasury of Medical Knowledge*, and more information on the NLM is available at www.nlm.nih.gov.

Regional Medical Library Program and National Network of Libraries of Medicine

In October 1965, the Medical Library Assistance Act established the Regional Medical Library Network. Now known as the National Network of Libraries of Medicine (NN/LM; nnlm.gov), this program is charged with "advanc[ing] the progress of medicine and improv[ing] the public health by providing all U.S. health professionals equal access to biomedical information and improving the public's access to information to enable them to make informed decisions about their health."[2] The NN/LM is coordinated by the NLM and has eight regional medical libraries that coordinate services for these regions:

- Middle Atlantic Region (Delaware, New Jersey, New York, Pennsylvania)

- Southeastern/Atlantic Region (Alabama, District of Columbia, Florida, Georgia, Maryland, Mississippi, North Carolina, Puerto Rico, South Carolina, Tennessee, Virginia, West Virginia, U.S. Virgin Islands)

- Greater Midwest Region (Illinois, Indiana, Iowa, Kentucky, Michigan, Minnesota, North Dakota, Ohio, South Dakota, Wisconsin)

- Midcontinental Region (Colorado, Kansas, Missouri, Nebraska, Utah, Wyoming)

- South Central Region (Arkansas, Louisiana, New Mexico, Oklahoma, Texas)

- Pacific Northwest Region (Alaska, Idaho, Montana, Oregon, Washington)

- Pacific Southwest Region (Arizona, California, Hawaii, Nevada, U.S. Territories in the Pacific Basin)

- New England Region (Connecticut, Maine, Massachusetts, New Hampshire, Rhode Island, Vermont)

The Armed Forces Medical Library (www.tricare.mil/afml) serves as the regional medical library for overseas military medical libraries.

In addition to resource sharing, NN/LM provides funding for outreach projects designed to enhance access to health information, as well as to a number of training and educational resources. Topics include providing consumer health information, serving Spanish speakers, grant and proposal writing, and using PubMed and other databases (more on PubMed in Chapter 5). A list of NN/LM's educational resources, including classes and handouts, is available at nnlm.gov/training, and more information on the NN/LM can be found at nnlm.gov.

Index-Catalogue and Index Medicus

In 1880, Dr. Billings began publishing the *Index-Catalogue*, an author and subject catalog of all the items in the Library of the Office of the Surgeon General. Billings received $20,000 from

Congress to fund the *Index-Catalogue*, a project he had begun five years earlier. Listing books, journal articles, theses, pamphlets, and more, the *Index-Catalogue* turned the library into a truly national library. Without its publication, the collection would have been used primarily by physicians living in Washington; before Billings took the helm, the Library of the Office of the Surgeon General was essentially for medical personnel only. When Billings began publishing the *Index-Catalogue* and the subsequent *Index Medicus*, however, "he addressed the need to access the current medical literature ... [and] provid[ed] relevant information to the medical profession."[3] When news of its publication hit, requests for copies of the *Index-Catalogue* came pouring in. As W. D. Miles writes, "A goodly portion of the medical literature of the world was opened to the physician who had access to the catalog. It saved the time of every researcher and directed him to writings he might not have found otherwise."[4] The *Index-Catalogue* ceased publication during World War II. Because the catalog took about 20 years to publish, references were not current, something physicians and researchers needed. (According to Miles, there would have been more than 3 million citations in the *Index-Catalogue* in 1960!) Indexing journals for the *Index-Catalogue* ended in March 1950.

The print precursor to MEDLINE (discussed in more detail in Chapter 5) is the *Index Medicus*. In 1879, Dr. Billings and the Library of the Office of the Surgeon General published a comprehensive index, the *Index Medicus*, of the medical journal articles available in the library. Though it began as an accompaniment to the *Index-Catalogue*, the *Index Medicus* soon became a popular and more successful publication. Whereas the *Index-Catalogue* was published just once per year, the *Index Medicus* was published monthly, providing current, up-to-date references to the medical literature. Billings began working on the subject index in January 1874, and the first issue was printed five years later. Billings employed library clerks and friends across the country to copy

English was always the only academic subject to completely capture my attention, so I earned a BS in English and communications from the University of Montevallo and later an MA in English from the University of Alabama. Right after [receiving] the master's degree, I took a grant writing position for a small nonprofit organization. Focusing on small opportunities for education and healthcare improvement, one grant in particular really made an impact. The mortality rates in West Alabama decreased as a direct result of training after we secured funding to teach health professionals about transferring pregnant women and new babies to larger facilities. I had always wanted to teach in some capacity, and seeing the large impact of such a small amount of training made an impression.

The small organization I was writing for could not fiscally handle many new projects, so I soon moved into a Medicaid billing position. A close friend had for years suggested I go into librarianship, but, not knowing about the opportunities and varied career paths of librarianship, I had consistently ignored him. When I realized I could be a teaching librarian, I earned an MLIS from the University of Alabama in one calendar year. Focusing on health sciences also came naturally, as I felt a sense of urgency to help increase and improve medical research. Dr. Steven MacCall served as an excellent mentor, encouraging and helping me learn this new field. He arranged an internship for me at the Lister Hill Library of the Health Sciences at the University of Alabama in Birmingham, where I followed individual librarians for one day each, learning their different roles and goals and how they all work together. Soon after graduation [Lister Hill Library] hired me to work part-time at the reference desk. This soon led to increased hours and benefits, and I looked up one day to discover I was a fully employed health sciences librarian.

I am from Alabama, and while I love Alabama, I hoped for a position that would take me places. In the summer of 2004, I interviewed and was hired as the Outreach Education Coordinator for the National Network of Libraries of Medicine, Southeastern/ Atlantic Region. We are a contract with the NLM held by the Health Sciences and Human Services Library at the University of Maryland, Baltimore. Our mission is to improve access to health information, and I teach and exhibit throughout the southeastern U.S., focusing on health professionals and academic and health sciences librarians but also working with many different people and groups. Travel does, at times, grow tiring, but I pull energy from those who share our goals and are working to effect change. Plus, teaching is often its own reward. We juggle many different responsibilities and wear multiple hats, from supervising funding and projects to organizing and serving on committees, all in an effort to meet the priorities and goals of the National Library of Medicine. I am consistently surprised at how happy I am to have an interesting, challenging, and fun career with a purpose.

Sheila Snow-Croft is Outreach Education Coordinator for the Regional Medical Library of the National Network of Libraries of Medicine, Southeastern/Atlantic Region (nnlm.gov/sea).

citations onto cards and mail these to him. Then Billings assigned a subject heading at the top of each card. Working on *Index Medicus* allowed Billings to develop and perfect his indexing classification system.

At the end of each year, the citations were compiled into the *Cumulated Index Medicus*. In 1927, the *Index Medicus* was merged with the *Quarterly Cumulative Index* (an index that formerly only included the most important journals) to form the *Quarterly Cumulative Index Medicus*. This new quarterly publication was published by the American Medical Association. NLM continued to publish *Index Medicus*, in some form or another, as a monthly subject and author guide until 2004. Today, though, the information that appeared in *Index Medicus* is available through the MEDLINE database. A brief history of both the *Index-Catalogue* and the *Index Medicus* appears in Frank R. Kellerman's *Introduction to Health Sciences Librarianship: A Management Handbook* as well as in Miles' work.

National Library of Medicine Classification System

Rather than using LC or Dewey, most medical and health sciences libraries classify their materials using the NLM Classification (originally the Army Medical Library Classification). Built on the work done by Billings, the NLM Classification was patterned after the LC system, which uses letters for broad subject categories and numbers to further subdivide them. This shelf classification system was developed at the end of World War II when the Rockefeller Foundation funded a team to devise a new system. The group considered using the LC schedule for medicine but determined that it would not be sufficient for the NLM's vast holdings.

The NLM Classification schedules are used with the LC schedules for general reference works and subjects related to medicine.

Each general topic includes related fields and specialties, as well as regions of the body that are associated with it. This basic outline is expanded to include the hierarchy within each specific schedule. Each schedule then begins with a list of numbers to further classify the types of publications—dictionaries, atlases, laboratory manuals, directories, handbooks, etc. A dictionary on pharmacology, for example, would be classified under QV 13. A book on the history of nursing would be classified under WY 11. Schedules QS–QZ and W–WZ are used to classify materials published after 1913. Works published from 1801 to 1913 are classified under the 19th Century Schedule, while materials published before 1801 are classified in WZ 220–270. For more information on the NLM Classification and practice, visit wwwcf.nlm.nih.gov/class/index.html.

Medical Subject Headings

Closely related to the NLM Classification are Medical Subject Headings (MeSH), the NLM's thesaurus of controlled vocabulary, which is used to index articles in PubMed and MEDLINE. Any health sciences librarian will need to be familiar with MeSH, "the keys that unlock the medical literature."[5] In 1947, the Army Medical Library held a meeting on medical subject headings, opening the session to other medical librarians for input. NLM first developed a *Subject Heading Authority List Used by the Current List Division Armed Forces Medical Library* in 1954 to categorize the primary headings and subheadings used. This list was printed for the first time in the 1960 *Medical Subject Headings* and contained just over 4,000 subject headings. Today there are more than 25,000 medical subject headings. In addition to the almost 5,000 biomedical journals indexed in PubMed and MEDLINE, MeSH is also used to index other medical and health sciences publications. The MeSH database can be searched online via the MeSH browser at www.nlm.nih.gov/mesh/MBrowser.html.

Preclinical Sciences

QS	Human Anatomy
QT	Physiology
QU	Biochemistry
QV	Pharmacology
QW	Microbiology and Immunology
QX	Parasitology
QY	Clinical Pathology
QZ	Pathology

Medicine and Related Subjects

W	Health Professions
WA	Public Health
WB	Practice of Medicine
WC	Communicable Diseases
WD	Disorders of Systemic, Metabolic, or Environmental Origin, etc.
WE	Musculoskeletal System
WF	Respiratory System
WG	Cardiovascular System
WH	Hemic and Lymphatic Systems
WI	Digestive System
WJ	Urogenital System
WK	Endocrine System
WL	Nervous System
WM	Psychiatry
WN	Radiology. Diagnostic Imaging
WO	Surgery
WP	Gynecology
WQ	Obstetrics
WR	Dermatology
WS	Pediatrics
WT	Geriatrics. Chronic Disease
WU	Dentistry. Oral Surgery
WV	Otolaryngology
WW	Ophthalmology
WX	Hospitals and Other Health Facilities
WY	Nursing
WZ	History of Medicine
19th Century Schedule	

Outline of NLM Classification

MeSH browser

Writing in 1964, Winifred Sewell, Deputy Chief of NLM's Bibliographic Services Division, compared subject headings to "directional signals or vectors, which, with other headings, serve to locate the essence of a particular paper or book in the universe of medical information."[6] MeSH provides a consistent method for finding information on a topic in which various terms and concepts may be used. While laypeople typically use the term *cancer*, articles in PubMed and MEDLINE will be indexed under *neoplasm*. A search of the MeSH database for *nosebleed* will map to *epistaxis*—defined as bleeding from the nose. It is really helpful to use MeSH when searching PubMed and MEDLINE because you can see the definition or scope note, cross references to previous terms and the years they were used, a list of subheadings, and a list of similar terms, as well as a MeSH tree.

MeSH in PubMed

The MeSH tree is arranged hierarchically by subject and is broken down into 16 main areas. Narrower, more specific terms are located under the broader terms. A search for *flu*, for example, maps to *influenza, human*. It is located under Virus Diseases and Respiratory Tract Diseases, which are both categorized under Diseases on the MeSH tree. Each MeSH term includes a set of entry terms or synonyms. Similar terms that might be used for flu are *human influenza*, *influenzas*, and *grippe*. Searching the MeSH database for any of these terms would map to the correct MeSH term of *influenza, human*.

MeSH includes a list of subheadings that can be used with each major heading. Also known as qualifiers, these terms are used to explain a specific aspect of the major heading. There are currently 83 subheadings that can be used with major subject headings.

A. Anatomy
B. Organisms
C. Diseases
D. Chemicals and Drugs
E. Analytical, Diagnostic, and Therapeutic Techniques and Equipment
F. Psychiatry and Psychology
G. Biological Sciences
H. Physical Sciences
I.   Anthropology, Education, Sociology, and Social Phenomena
J.   Technology and Food and Beverages
K. Humanities
L. Information Science
M. Health Care
V. Publication Characteristics
Z. Geographic Locations

MeSH tree structure

Examples of possible subheadings include *contraindications, etiology, methods,* and *prevention and control.* A list of subheadings accompanies all terms in the MeSH database.

In addition to major headings and subheadings, the MeSH database includes publication characteristics. Rather than describing the content or topic of the publication, these terms describe the type of publication (e.g., letter, clinical trial, or research study). The publication type category is divided into three primary sections: publication components, publication format, and study characteristics. *Journal article* is probably the most frequently used publication format.

MeSH terminology was enhanced in the 1960s with the development of MEDLARS (Medical Literature Analysis and Retrieval System). Author Cheryl Dee writes that "by 1964 the rapid advances in biomedical sciences created some deficiencies in [MeSH] use," so NLM worked to "enrich the MeSH terminology with the latest medical concepts."[7] Each year, when a new MeSH is published, so is a list of added, changed, or deleted descriptors. Medical terminology changes rapidly, so in an attempt to include emerging concepts, the MeSH terms are modified on a regular basis. NLM staff have to be careful, however, that terms are not added too soon or too late to keep current. MeSH, including terminology changes, was printed each year until 2007. Today, MeSH is available online via the MeSH Browser and PubMed, where files are updated every week.

For more information on MeSH and how to search with MeSH, consult The Basics of Medical Subject Headings at www.nlm.nih.gov/bsd/disted/mesh. Branching Out: The MeSH Vocabulary, an online video tutorial (www.nlm.nih.gov/bsd/ disted/video), is also extremely helpful in understanding and using MeSH.

I believe health sciences librarianship is a natural fit for me because I used to be a nurse. When I hear a nursing student talking about giving that first injection, I can relate to that; I remember it—but when I was working toward my library degree, I had not decided on a library career path. Since health sciences librarianship was a strong possibility, I took a class in medical librarianship. As part of my coursework I completed a collection development project for a small nursing library and learned about searching the health sciences literature. I enjoyed the class and related activities tremendously.

Now that I am a practicing health and life sciences librarian, I continue to enjoy what I am doing. Sure, there are challenges, the greatest of which revolve around time. There is never enough time to do everything I need to do and want to do! I work in an academic library, and it can get very busy, especially during fall semester. During the summer, though, our teaching

activities drop, and I use some of that extra time to prepare new classes. Right now I am developing a work-
shop on finding information about heritable single
gene disorders in humans using OMIM (Online
Mendelian Inheritance in Man) and PubMed.

The most rewarding aspects of my job have to do
with the variety of my job—from developing and teaching library workshops for undergraduate nursing students to planning and teaching a library session for
graduate biology students to staffing the reference desk
to analyzing our health and life sciences collection. But
out of all that, I would say the most rewarding part of
my job is interacting with our students. Working with a
first semester nursing student and helping that student
mature into a more independent learner gives me a
great deal of satisfaction.

If this sounds like the kind of work you would like to
do, take a class or classes in health sciences librarianship. Intern or volunteer at a health sciences or life sciences library. Become familiar with the terminology.
Attend a local conference, read the journal literature,
and talk to other health sciences librarians to find out
what they do, and what challenges and satisfactions
they experience.

*Suzanne Stemler is Nursing & Health Studies, Life
Sciences, Chemistry, & Environmental Studies Librarian
at the University of Miami's Richter Library (www.library.
miami.edu) in Coral Gables, Florida.*

Cumulative Index to Nursing and Allied Health Literature Headings

Another tool to be aware of is Cumulative Index to Nursing and Allied Health Literature (CINAHL) subject headings. CINAHL headings follow the same tree structure as MeSH. Today there are more than 12,000 CINAHL headings used to index the materials included in the CINAHL database. A total of 68 topical subheadings can be used in conjunction with the CINAHL headings. While many of these subheadings are the same as MeSH subheadings, not all of them match the MeSH terms. Some, such as nursing theory, are unique to CINAHL. CINAHL headings specific to nursing include North American Nursing Diagnosis Association (NANDA) nursing diagnoses terms, IOWA Nursing Interventions Classifications terms, and Saba Clinical Care Classification terms for diagnoses and interventions, major nursing models, and nursing specialties.

As with MeSH, CINAHL indexers also assign publication types. Called document types, these terms describe the type and format of the publications. In addition, indexers note special features such as test questions, care plans, sample forms, or practice guidelines. CINAHL subject headings also contain special subject headings for nursing diagnoses and classifications. When looking for articles on nursing and allied health topics, CINAHL is a great place to start.[8]

For more information on CINAHL and CINAHL headings, view the Using CINAHL Headings tutorial created at the Duke University Medical Center Library (www.mclibrary.duke.edu/training/cinahl headings). You may also want to take a look at Searching CINAHL with Subject Headings, developed at the McGoogan Library of Medicine at the University of Nebraska Medical Center (app1.unmc.edu/mcgoogan/guides/CINAHL/headings.html), and check out the CINAHL Support Center (support.ebsco.com/cinahl), which contains help sheets and FAQs.

CINAHL headings

Medical Terminology

One of the hardest parts of being a new health sciences librarian is figuring out all of the terminology. In her book *Health Information on the Internet*, Rowena Cullen notes that physicians' searching of MEDLINE was "hampered by a lack of understanding of Medical Subject Headings (MeSH) and how the MeSH thesaurus is applied."[9] When planning a "Mini-Medical School for Librarians" in 2000/2001, "the language or terminology on which medicine is based" was one of the five content areas for the program.[10] While a course in anatomy and physiology might be ideal for learning such things, it is not always practical. So where can a new health sciences librarian learn all of this? A great deal is learned on the job, just by observing and listening to users' requests. You might also find it helpful to browse through medical dictionaries or basic medical or biology textbooks. *Dorland's Illustrated Medical Dictionary* and *Stedman's Medical Dictionary* are good choices for general information, but, depending on the topic and the type of library, other sources may need to be consulted. See the "Medical Terminology" chapter in *Introduction to Reference Sources in the Health Sciences* for more suggestions.

There is also a wealth of information available on the internet. The Medical Library Association (MLA) offers a "Deciphering

Medspeak" pamphlet, which defines a number of commonly used medical terms. In addition, MLA publishes "Rx Riddles Solved!" to translate prescription shorthand and "Deciphering Medspeak" brochures on specific diseases such as breast cancer, diabetes, and HIV-AIDS. Find all of these publications on the MLA website at www.mlanet.org/resources/medspeak. Many colleges and universities also provide medical terminology courses; Des Moines University, for instance, offers a free online medical terminology course at www.dmu.edu/medterms. The medical encyclopedia and dictionary available from the NLM's MedlinePlus (medline plus.gov) are also valuable resources.

Medical terminology involves more than just the names of diseases, procedures, and body parts. The jargon also includes organizations, journals, people, and more—and almost everything has an acronym. The *Journal of the American Medical Association*, for example, is known simply as *JAMA*, while AHIP stands for the Academy of Health Information Professionals. These acronyms can sometimes be misleading. For instance, MLA stands for the Medical Library Association—as well as for the Music Library Association and the Modern Language Association. In her book *A Medical Librarian?—What's That?*, Ilona von Magyary-Kossa remembers when she was a new librarian and a physician asked her for recent issues of *JAMA*, "the green journal," and the "Procsoc." Having no idea what he was referring to, she was embarrassed when a colleague knew right away that the doctor wanted "some of the most widely read medical journals."[11] In situations like this, remember that your colleagues and other health sciences librarians can be a tremendous source of information. (See more on networking and training in Chapter 6.) Don't be afraid to ask for help and admit when you are unsure of something.

The importance of learning the medical terminology was a pervasive theme throughout the responses to the Accidental

Health Sciences Librarian survey. Many respondents mentioned that individuals interested in a career as a health sciences librarian should take a course in health sciences librarianship as well as a course in a health science. Even though just over 10 percent of respondents held a degree in a health sciences field, many felt that a second degree in the health sciences would be beneficial. One person wrote that it was important "to learn the language of medical terminology," while another stated that new health sciences librarians should take a course in medical terminology if their degrees were not in the health field. It is evident from these responses that understanding the medical vocabulary is an important asset for any health sciences librarian. Respondents all felt that it was necessary to have a solid understanding of MeSH. One respondent summed it up best, saying that future health sciences librarians must "get comfortable with medical terminology and cozy with MeSH!"

No matter what niche of health sciences librarianship you choose, you will need to learn the terminology. (For some terminology, see the glossary at the end.) In some cases you'll also need to learn the institution-specific terminology that your library uses. Getting comfortable with the vocabulary will help when you're starting out in any field. Keep in mind that many health sciences subfields also have their own terminology and jargon. We always recommend that you don't assume that a widget to you is a widget to a doctor or nurse—they might call it a whatzit—so be sure you don't run into communication issues because you aren't familiar with the specific terminology. Keep a few relevant dictionaries nearby and bookmarked.

Endnotes

1. Title 42, Chapter 6A, Subchapter III, Part D, Subpart 1, §286 National Library of Medicine.

2. National Network of Libraries of Medicine website, "About the National Network of Libraries of Medicine," nnlm.gov/about

3. Frances K. Groen, *Access to Medical Knowledge: Libraries, Digitization, and the Public Good* (Lanham, MD: Scarecrow Press, 2007), 28.

4. Wyndham D. Miles, *A History of the National Library of Medicine: The Nation's Treasury of Medical Knowledge* (Washington, DC: Government Printing Office, 1982), 130.

5. Margaret H. Coletti and Howard L. Bleich, "Medical Subject Headings Used to Search the Biomedical Literature," *Journal of the American Medical Informatics Association* 8, no. 4 (July/Aug. 2001): 1.

6. Winifred Sewell, "Medical Subject Headings in MEDLARS," *Bulletin of the Medical Library Association* 52, no. 1 (Jan. 1964): 164.

7. Cheryl Rae Dee, "The Development of the Medical Literature Analysis and Retrieval System (MEDLARS)," *Journal of the Medical Library Association* 95, no. 4 (Oct. 2007): 419.

8. For more information on CINAHL, see the publisher's website at www.ebscohost.com/cinahl or Maureen (Molly) Knapp, "CINAHL Plus," *Journal of the Medical Library Association* 94, no. 3 (July 2006): 355–356.

9. Rowena Cullen, *Health Information on the Internet: A Study of Providers, Quality, and Users* (Westport, CT: Praeger, 2006), 127.

10. Kathel Dunn, Suzanne J. Crow, T. Guillaume Van Moorsel, Jeannine Creazzo, Patricia Tomasulo, and Andrea Markinson, "Mini-Medical School for Librarians: From Needs Assessment to Educational Outcomes," *Journal of the Medical Library Association* 94, no. 2 (Apr. 2006): 168.

11. Ilona von Magyary-Kossa, *A Medical Librarian?—What's That?* (Jericho, NY: Exposition Press, 1974), 24.

Chapter 3

It's All About the People

> *I have the opportunity to touch so many lives every day, by offering information from a number of resources to patients, family members, and employees, which helps them to make wise healthcare decisions and reinforces their ability to ask appropriate questions regarding their care.*
>
> —Survey Respondent

No matter what niche of health sciences librarianship you end up in, it's all about the people—and this is especially true in public services. When we moved to a health sciences library from a medium-sized liberal arts college, we were surprised to discover that the range of topics and variety of users did not shrink but actually expanded. We didn't need to worry that the health sciences focus of the library would be narrow or get boring. One day we may be helping first-year nursing students learn the basics of CINAHL, and the next we may be helping hardcore researchers working on an experimental treatment for rheumatoid arthritis, helping a consumer health patron looking up the best treatment for poison ivy, or helping a local high school student working on a science fair project.

While in many respects public services in health sciences libraries mirrors public services in any library, the health sciences environment creates some unique issues. While a complete "how-to" for health sciences public services is beyond the scope of this book, we'll talk here about the aspects we found the most challenging and interesting. We hope to help you avoid the culture shock we experienced! If you're looking for more information, *Introduction to Reference Sources in the Health Sciences* (2008) is the best go-to source for information on all aspects of reference sources, covering collection development and management as well as bibliographic and information sources.

Reference

How you "do reference" in a health sciences library depends largely on which type of patrons you are helping and their information needs. Consumer health patrons have vastly different needs from doctors, who have very different needs from nursing students. No matter what, the basics of the reference interview you learned about in library school still apply—but we recommend that, before you get started, you 1) find out what kind of patron you are helping and what their information need is and 2) ask whether this information is for personal use, for a class, or for research. Those two pieces of information are key to how you will proceed.

For example, suppose someone comes in asking for information on a rare and fatal disease. Since this person is wearing a white coat, you assume she is a clinician. You proceed to find all sorts of articles that dramatically outline how horrible this disease is—and she bursts into tears because a family member has just been diagnosed with it. You then find out that, instead of working with a doctor, you are actually talking to a nutritionist who came over on her lunch hour to get consumer information for her family member. You just got the patron type and information need wrong. While you should strive to avoid these kinds of assumptions in any library setting, in health sciences you will only make this mistake once.

Consumer Health: You Need a License to Practice Medicine

One of the most important things to remember when working in a health sciences library is that you *cannot* dispense medical advice! Your job is to provide unbiased health and medical information. Patrons will often ask you what doctor they should see or what procedure they should have. In fact, it isn't all that unusual for someone to come to the information desk and show you exactly what they are talking about—whether it be a rash, injury, or other symptom. Even though you may very well recognize their affliction as a raging case of poison ivy, you *must not* diagnose it. Not only is it illegal for you to do so, it is dangerous. One survey respondent mentioned that one of the hardest things to do is "make sure I don't cross the ethical line between giving information and giving advice when answering patron questions." Most librarians have had no medical training, and we are not health-care providers.

While it may seem like common sense that you should not diagnose patrons' illnesses, you should also be careful about dispensing any sort of medical advice. Patrons will also ask questions such as "Who is the best doctor to see about ...?" or "Do you think I should have this surgery/procedure and/or take this drug?" Never recommend a specific physician or hospital. There are plenty of resources that give patrons information on individual physicians or hospitals, such as *Hospital Statistics*, *Profiles of U.S. Hospitals*, and *Physician Characteristics & Distribution in the U.S.* Often just explaining that you aren't a doctor and can't give medical advice will suffice, and there isn't any harm in encouraging folks to visit a doctor, either. You'll also want to have a medical dictionary on hand for users who might ask you to explain or interpret medical concepts and terms.

When working with consumer health patrons, you may also find it harder to elicit needed information from them. Generally

speaking, when you are working with consumers, they need information because they or someone they care about is sick. The illness or condition could be devastating, it could just be
embarrassing, they may not have understood what the doctor was
telling them (more on this later in the chapter), or it may be a combination of these factors. In her article about working with patrons
with mental illnesses, Michelle L. Eberle offers good advice that
can be applied to any consumer health encounter in which the
person is nervous, agitated, or stressed (and the patron usually is
all three).[1] Eberle recommends maintaining a list of open-ended
questions in your bag of tricks to get folks to talk comfortably with
you. For examples of open-ended questions, go to infopeople.org/
training/past/2004/reference/open-ended_questions.pdf. As you
work more with consumers, however, you will find that you
develop a style and technique all your own.

If possible, work with people in a private space—not so private
that you feel threatened in any way, but even just a quiet corner
may give the person enough privacy to feel OK about talking
about the issue or even to get emotional. If you do find yourself
in the middle of a gut-wrenching situation, remind the patron—
and yourself—that any information you find may or may not
apply to the patient's specific situation. Often medical literature
is either very general or very specific. Medical outcomes depend
on a complex mix of ingredients, including such things as medical history, age, willingness to participate in treatment, and
overall health. Encourage patrons to take the information you
find back to their doctor so that they can go over it together. Also,
remember to keep a professional distance. In many respects,
working with consumer health patrons is one of the most rewarding aspects of health sciences librarianship, but it also is the most
emotional.

Another topic that consumer health librarians regularly tackle is
health information literacy. In a nutshell, health information literacy

refers to a person's ability to find health information, understand it, and use it to make better health-related decisions. Sadly, the vast majority of adults lack the basic skills needed to manage their health and avoid disease.[2] This topic has received a good bit of attention. It seems that no matter where you turn these days, you are inundated with health information, from television shows like *Diagnosis X* and *Dr. G: Medical Examiner* to a whole host of magazines to interactive websites like WebMD. All of these resources are contributing to an increased awareness of health information literacy—or the lack of it.

One of the most important aspects of health information literacy being addressed today focuses on how physicians communicate with their patients. You often have just a short time with the doctor, and during that time you are hit with a large amount of information that you are expected to not only remember but understand. No matter how educated or literate you are, medical terminology is hard. Add to that the general reluctance of patients to ask questions, and it is no wonder patrons come to librarians scared and confused. Part of your role as consumer health librarian is to turn *pharmacokinetics* into *how this drug works* and *angina* into *chest pain*. Bridging that language barrier is an important aspect of working with consumer health patients, and it applies to working with the doctors, too. Consumer health librarians can often be found working with healthcare providers, teaching them about health information literacy issues and how to use consumer health resources.

It is important that consumer health librarians also get out of the physical library to do their work. They don't wait for consumers to come to them, and they don't make healthcare providers come to the library, either. You can find consumer health librarians at all sorts of events, from health fairs to church outreach activities to medical conferences. Luckily, if you accidentally find yourself in the role of consumer health librarian, there are tons of great resources. Here is a sampling of some of our favorites.

Michele Spatz's *Answering Consumer Health Questions: The Medical Library Association Guide for Reference Librarians* is recommended reading for all health sciences librarians, both new and experienced. This work deals with all aspects of delivering consumer health information, from ethics and legal issues to dealing with difficult patrons. Interspersed throughout are what the author calls "exhibits"—recommended resources, tips, and templates.

The term *accidental* health sciences librarian fits me to a *T*. When I was laid off in late 2006 after 15 years in corporate information centers, I spoke to an SLA [Special Libraries Association] colleague who was moving and submitted my resume for the job she was leaving. A few months later, I was the new director of a small consumer health library. I am happy to report that not only did I survive my first year, but I love it!

One of the best things about librarianship is that we can take our experience and skills from one arena into another. The years I spent doing business research, working on project teams, assessing new databases and products, and interacting with many different people and personalities have all been very valuable and transferable to my present job.

My library is not easily categorized. It is a "public library," funded by property taxes and administered by a local government agency, but it is not part of the city or county library systems. It is a "special library" because of its subject focus. It is a "health sciences library," but it is not part of the local hospital. Our collection includes books, journals, videos, and online resources, all focused on healthcare for consumers and patients.

Working with people who need health or medical information is definitely the most rewarding aspect of my job. It is so gratifying to know that we have been able to help them find information for themselves or a loved one to better understand a disease or condition, upcoming surgery, diagnosis, or medication.

Of course, there have been some challenges along the way. Collection development has been one of the biggest, but there are many tools, resources, and mentors to help with that. Serving the public is certainly different from doing research for corporate colleagues, but it is very rewarding. An ongoing challenge is doing outreach and marketing to let the community know about this wonderful free resource. On the plus side, I inherited three skilled library assistants who have been generous in sharing their experience and knowledge with me.

I would encourage anyone interested in a career in health sciences librarianship to go for it! If possible, take a class to give you a basic understanding of the field, but if you know how to do research, collection development, and cataloging, you can transfer those skills from one type of library to another. Be sure to join the Medical Library Association (MLA) and SLA and tap into the resources and people available to help you.

Kathy Quinn is Library Director of the Dr. William C. Herrick Community Health Care Library (www.herrick library.org) in La Mesa, California.

For consumer health questions, be aware of the National Network of Libraries of Medicine (NN/LM) site on the Consumer Health Reference Interview and Ethical Issues (nnlm.gov/out reach/consumer/ethics.html). These guidelines can generally be used for any reference interview. Readers may also be interested in the podcast of "I Don't Give Medical Advice; I Dispense Quality Health Information" (infopeople.org/training/webcasts/web cast_data/242).

The University of Connecticut Health Center Library's Healthnet: Connecticut Consumer Health Information Network maintains a list of recommended books for libraries that answer consumer health questions. Available at library.uchc.edu/departm/hnet/corelist.html, this list includes directories, encyclopedias, and bibliographies as well as books in specific categories such as aging, drugs, and mental health. Healthnet has also developed a list of magazines and newsletters (library.uchc.edu/departm/hnet/nlist.html) and internet resources (library.uchc.edu/departm/hnet/inters.html) for consumer health and public libraries. In addition, Healthnet has drafted some guidelines for providing consumer health information (library.uchc.edu/departm/hnet/guidelines.html).

One of the most helpful resources for librarians answering consumer health questions is MedlinePlus (www.medlineplus.gov). Started in 1998, MedlinePlus compiles information from the National Library of Medicine (NLM), the National Institutes of Health (NIH), and various other medical organizations on more than 750 diseases. MedlinePlus also includes directories, an encyclopedia, a dictionary, tutorials, drug information, recent news, links to clinical trials, and preformulated MEDLINE searches on a number of topics. For more information on MedlinePlus, see the interactive tour at www.nlm.nih.gov/medlineplus/tour/medline plustour.html. We've both found MedlinePlus to be an indispensable go-to resource when working with consumer health patrons.

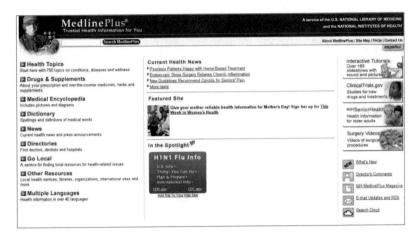

MedlinePlus

The Consumer Health Manual (nnlm.gov/outreach/consumer) from the NN/LM is a wonderful resource. It discusses starting a consumer health library, conducting the reference interview, evaluating websites, seeking out funding opportunities, and even best practices in designing a consumer health website. Also check out the MLA's Consumer and Patient Health Information Section (CAPHIS) and its policy statement on the Librarian's Role in the Provision of Consumer Health Information and Patient Education (caphis.mlanet.org/chis/librarian.html). CAPHIS maintains an entire section on managing a consumer health information library, with resources on planning, budgeting, staff, collection development, reference, and more. CAPHIS also publishes a list of 100 trustworthy health and medical websites. Lastly, the fall 2004 issue, "Strategic Strides Toward a Better Future," and the winter 2005 issue, "Consumer Health Issues, Trends, and Research," of *Library Trends* have a number of interesting articles on the topic of consumer health.

MLA has also recently started a Consumer Health Information Specialization (CHIS) program. Available to health professionals as well as to librarians who work with consumers, this specialization is intended to provide members with information on new resources and "help members obtain an additional level of expertise in the area of consumer health information."[3] More information on the CHIS program can be found at www.mlanet.org/education/chc.

The People

Students

The types of students you will come into contact with as a health sciences librarian are extremely varied. We generally deal with nursing and optometry students since those are our respective liaison areas, but when working the information desk, we can encounter students ranging from entering freshmen to medical residents. Since we came from an academic environment, neither of us noticed much that we needed to do differently when working with students.

We did notice, however, that the students were a bit different. For instance, the various entering classes of health sciences students tend to go through a very rigid program as a cohort. Also, given the time health sciences students must spend in the lab or in clinical rotations, they have very little free time to come to the library. As a result we spend a good bit of time helping these students via email—or if email just isn't working, we let them choose a time that is convenient for them to come into the library. As long as the library is open, we are willing to meet. Health sciences students tend be highly focused and driven, but we still get some students that wait until the last minute to do their research. Overall, though, students are students. If you love working with students, you'll really enjoy working with health sciences students.

Clinicians and Clinical Medical Librarians/Informationists

You will notice right off that clinicians, any kind of clinician, have very little time for research. As one article points out, "Physicians don't, and never will, have that kind of time to look for the answers to most of their clinical questions themselves."[4] One way librarians have sought to help meet the needs of clinicians is with clinical medical librarian programs. In addition to providing information to physicians more rapidly and at the point of care, clinical medical librarian programs seek to put librarians on the clinician's healthcare team. That means that a librarian goes on rounds and sits in while clinicians discuss patient care.

Librarian Gertrude Lamb established the first clinical medical librarian program in 1971 at the University of Missouri–Kansas City School of Medicine. When clinical medical librarian programs started, many used LATCH (literature attached to charts) in which articles relating to a patient's condition were attached to his or her chart. Librarians would attend morning reports with the healthcare team, then return to the library to do research on any questions that had arisen. They would print the relevant articles and deliver them to the team the next morning. While the use of LATCH has virtually disappeared, the role of clinical medical librarians has only increased over the years. Today clinical librarians may go on rounds, educate healthcare professionals on how to search for evidence and information on their own, participate in hospital or clinical committees, and much more.

While the traditional clinical librarian typically found literature pertaining to the patient's condition, the new informationist is a part of the healthcare team who "provide[s] appropriate literature for decision-making but also participate[s] in teaching, filtering, and evaluating the literature, as well as creating specialty knowledge databases for the care team."[5] The Eskind Biomedical Library (EBL) at the Vanderbilt University Medical Center has developed a new approach to clinical librarianship. In their article "Evolution of a Mature Clinical Informationist Model," Nunzia B. Guise et al. note that the clinical informationist model at EBL "assumes that (1) informationists, equipped with extensive, relevant clinical knowledge and an understanding of research practices, can deliver highly targeted evidence in support of patient care and (2) the integration of evidence identified by human insight and intelligence with informatics tools provides an efficient and effective mechanism for making relevant information available when and where clinical decisions are made."[6] As they point out, the EBL model, known as the Clinical Informatics Consult Service (CICS), "integrates librarians into clinical rounding teams as expert information providers, equipped with adequately deep background knowledge in both principles of clinical medicine and information seeking. CICS participants can diagnose unexpressed information needs as they occur during practice and prepare relevant, balanced syntheses of the evidence from the medical literature."[7] For more information on the CICS program, see www.mc.vanderbilt.edu/biolib/services/cics.html.

Working with and reaching clinicians can be difficult, but once you start to establish relationships it can be very rewarding. You will actively be participating in patient care. You could be making a difference in someone's treatment. How exciting is that?!

Researchers

Just as with health sciences students, researchers in health sciences are like most other researchers. They are in it for the long haul, and when they say they want everything on topic X, they really want *everything* on that topic. One major difference we noticed, however, is that many of the researchers in health sciences are paid to do research and to do it within a certain time frame. In this way, they differ from history professors who conduct long-term research projects as part of their job or in order to get a promotion or tenure. For researchers in health sciences, research *is* their job! Further, generally their research will be funded by a grant of some sort. That means they have special rules to follow and very strict deadlines. These types of researchers also tend to be very focused on watching what is being published right now. While historical data is important, the more recent stuff is more important—especially if there is a new development. We've seen librarians get totally sucked into some serious research projects, and this is a good thing. Not only did the librarians become part of the research team, but they also eventually were listed as co-authors on the publication.

Areas to Watch

Evidence-Based Medicine

One of the hottest topics in health sciences librarianship today is evidence-based medicine (EBM). One of the most common definitions of EBM is "the conscientious, explicit and judicious use of current best evidence in making decisions about the care of the individual patient. It means integrating individual clinical expertise with the best available external clinical evidence from systematic research."[8] Two survey respondents also summed up EBM nicely: "[ensuring] that patients' rights are upheld and that health professionals have timely access to the most accurate/up-to-date evidence-based information available" and "keeping the intellectual rigor in the systematic evidence-based approach in the face of poor information literacy, federated search and Google." In a nutshell, EBM takes the best medical evidence, clinical expertise, and the patient's wishes, and factors them all into the patient care decision process. While practicing clinicians are usually the ones pursuing EBM information, you will also need to be familiar with the concepts if you deal with students.

You can find a number of freely available tutorials on EBM on the web. Two of the best are Introduction to Evidence-Based Medicine from the Duke University Medical Center Library and the Health Sciences Library at the University of North Carolina–Chapel Hill (www.hsl.unc.edu/Services/Tutorials/EBM) and Evidence-Based Practice: An Interprofessional Tutorial from the University of Minnesota Bio-Medical Library (www.biomed.lib.umn.edu/learn/ebp). Introduction to Evidence-Based Medicine is a self-paced tutorial that provides users with the basic concepts of EBM, including how to construct a clinical question, search strategies, and evaluating the evidence.

Essentially, there are five steps to evidence-based practice:

1. Define the question.

2. Gather the evidence.

3. Evaluate the evidence.

4. Apply the evidence.

5. Evaluate the whole process.

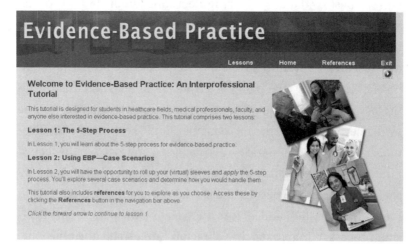

Evidence-based practice tutorial from the
University of Minnesota Bio-Medical Library

When formulating a clinical question, keep in mind the acronym PICO, which stands for:

P = Patient or problem

I = Intervention (or cause/prognosis)

C = Comparison intervention (what alternatives could be used)

O = Outcomes

The University of South Carolina School of Medicine Library has also developed a good EBM tutorial that takes users through the steps of forming a clinical question and locating the evidence (uscm.med.sc.edu/ebmtutorial). It is divided into six modules, and there are review questions at the end of each.

Evidence-Based Medicine Resources Tutorial

Introduction to EBM Resources	5 min.
Accessing EBM Resources	2 min.
The Cochrane Library	10 min.
Essential Evidence Plus	5 min.
National Guideline Clearinghouse	5 min.
Ovid MEDLINE	7 min.

There are six tutorial modules.

During the modules, you will be prompted to click links, type searches, and answer questions.

You can move through the tutorial sequentially or view individual modules separately.

If you have any questions or comments about this tutorial, please contact:

Roz Anderson
roz.anderson@uscmed.sc.edu
803-733-3310

University of South Carolina School of Medicine Library

Evidence-based medicine tutorial from the
University of South Carolina School of Medicine Library

While EBM is one of the best ways to ensure that patients are provided with the best possible care, practitioners often are unsure how to incorporate EBM and do not understand how to do literature searches or how to use the databases and resources or read research articles. One of our survey participants wrote, "Getting them [clinicians] to a) understand the importance of EBM, b) take the time to search the latest literature, etc., and c) actually base their treatment on what they find is one of the biggest hurdles." Another mentioned that one of the most significant aspects of her job is "helping nursing students and faculty in their search for information, and incorporating critical thinking skills in this, leading to evidence-based practice. It is inspiring to be able to contribute to the care of patients through my work with nursing students and faculty."

We've noticed lots of confusion and uncertainty about EBM, but luckily there are lots of good resources if you are interested or need to learn more. For instance, librarian Cleo Pappas' "Evidence-Based Medicine: An Overview and Teaching Tips" should be required reading for anyone interested in learning more about EBM.[9] Pappas gives an overview and history of EBM in addition to pointing readers to various EBM resources and teaching approaches. Although it is written for orthopedic nurses, librarians will also find useful Susan W. Salmond's article "Advancing Evidence-Based Practice: A Primer," which provides a good introduction to EBM, including barriers to EBM, the EBM "skill set," and the levels of evidence such as practice guidelines, systematic reviews, and randomized controlled trials. Salmond also provides a chart illustrating how to ask a PICO question.[10] Dartmouth College hosts Supporting Clinical Care: An Institute in Evidence-Based Practice for Medical Librarians (see www.dartmouth.edu/~biomed/institute2009). When you are just starting out, though, just being able to define EBM puts you ahead of where we were when we began our stint as health sciences librarians.

Systematic Reviews and Expert Searches

Another aspect of health sciences librarianship you might run up against is systematic reviews. And they are hard! A systematic review is essentially a review of all the studies on a specific, clinical question. An editorial in *Annals of Internal Medicine* defines systematic reviews as "concise summaries of the best available evidence that address sharply defined clinical questions." The authors go on to say that "although it looks easy from the outside, producing a high-quality systematic review is extremely demanding. The realization of how difficult the task is should be reassuring to all of us who have been frustrated by our seeming inability to stay informed and up to date by combing through the literature ourselves."[11]

In 1997, the *Annals of Internal Medicine* published a series of articles on systematic reviews with information on what they are, how to find and use them, and how to conduct them. In the first article of the series, the authors provide an overview of systematic reviews and how they differ from other types of reviews. They go on to say that "investigators need systematic reviews to summarize existing data, refine hypotheses, estimate sample sizes, and help define future research agendas. Without systematic reviews, researchers may miss promising leads or may embark on studies of questions that have been already answered."[12] The second article in the series delves into the process for finding and appraising systematic reviews. MEDLINE/PubMed and the Cochrane Library are two of the best sources for locating systematic reviews.

A more recent article in the *Journal of the Medical Library Association*, "Systematic Reviews Need Systematic Searchers," looks at the ways in which health sciences librarians can contribute to systematic reviews. The authors discuss the reference interview, developing the search, and the search strategy itself. They point out that searching multiple databases is best since different databases employ various indexing techniques. A search in

MEDLINE, for instance, may produce different results from the same search in another database. The authors also mention that "a comprehensive selection of sources for a systematic review often includes two or more bibliographic databases such as MEDLINE and EMBASE, a trials registry, conference proceedings, specialized subject bibliographies, reference lists of review articles, and contact with researchers and companies working in the area."[13]

Possibilities abound for librarian involvement in the systematic review process. Librarians can conduct instruction sessions or develop tutorials on how to search various databases, help locate grey literature like conference proceedings and reports, or educate researchers on citation management software. One survey respondent mentioned that he/she is "constantly challenged to become better at reference, information seeking, and evaluating the ever growing medical literature." Another wrote that she "love[s] being able to contribute to the work of a physician or researcher."

Those interested in learning more about systematic reviews and searching may also be interested in learning more about expert searching. The *MLA News* periodically publishes articles about expert searching in order to keep readers up to date and aware of new tools. MLA's Policy Statement on the Role of Expert Searching in Health Sciences Libraries may also be beneficial reading, as well as its Expert Searching list. All are available at www.mlanet.org/ resources/expert_search. You may also want to take a look at the book *The MLA Essential Guide to Becoming an Expert Searcher: Proven Techniques, Strategies, and Tips for Finding Health Information,* by Terry Ann Jankowski. Jankowski, a librarian at the University of Washington's Health Sciences Library, includes checklists, guidelines, and exercises for becoming an expert searcher in finding health information.

NIH Public Access Policy

The NIH policy states:

> The Director of the National Institutes of Health shall require that all investigators funded by the NIH submit or have submitted for them to the National Library of Medicine's PubMed Central an electronic version of their final, peer-reviewed manuscripts upon acceptance for publication, to be made publicly available no later than 12 months after the official date of publication: Provided, That the NIH shall implement the public access policy in a manner consistent with copyright law.[14]

Basically, the NIH Public Access Policy ensures that the public has access to the published results of NIH-funded research. Implementing Division G, Title II, Section 218 of PL 110-161 (Consolidated Appropriations Act, 2008), the policy requires researchers to deposit their final peer-reviewed journal manuscripts with PubMed Central once the paper has been accepted for publication. Papers must be made available to the public through PubMed Central within 12 months of publication. PubMed Central is the NIH's free digital collection of biomedical and life sciences journal literature, and content in PubMed Central is available at www.pubmedcentral.nih.gov.

Depending on the type of library, the NIH Public Access Policy may have little or no impact. However, in academic and research institutions, librarians may have to deal with this policy (on a daily basis), answering questions or providing assistance to researchers. A quick look at various health sciences library websites shows that a number of libraries have presented information about the NIH Public Access Policy, including recent news, tutorials, and help with the manuscript submission process. The library at the University of Texas Health Science Center–San Antonio has created a video explaining the policy and steps researchers should take (www.library.uthscsa.edu/university/nihpinch.cfm). The University of Alabama at Birmingham's Lister Hill Library of the Health Sciences has a number of tutorials and has even developed a submission system (www.uab.edu/lister/faq/index.php?askReference ID=3&action=category&c=22) using Microsoft's SharePoint that allows researchers to submit their papers to the library, which then submits the papers to PubMed Central. Both the policy and the submission process are straightforward and simple, so you just need to be aware of the policy and your library's role in helping people submit their research. More information about the NIH Public Access Policy can be found at publicaccess.nih.gov.

Informatics

At first glance, informatics doesn't seem that much different from what librarians do every day. Both deal with information and technology, but there are some important differences. First, keep in mind that informatics is relatively new. The term originated in the 1960s, as a combination of the words *information* and *automatic*, and there is more than one accepted definition of informatics. Broadly speaking, informatics uses information science, information processing, and information systems to examine and study both natural and artificial systems that store, process, access, and communicate information. In general, an informatics program will require many more computer science courses than an LIS degree does, as well as coursework in system and database administration.

The broad field of informatics can be narrowed down to discipline-specific concentrations, such as bioinformatics for molecular biology, medical or health informatics for healthcare, and nursing informatics. The American Medical Informatics Association (www.amia.org) provides a comprehensive definition for health/medical informatics on its website, saying that it "combines health sciences ... with computer science, management and decision science, biostatistics, engineering and information technology [to solve] problems in healthcare delivery, pharmaceutical, biomedical and health sciences research, health education and clinical/medical decision making."[15]

The National Library of Medicine sponsors an annual fellowship program in biomedical informatics at the Marine Biological Laboratory in Woods Hole, Massachusetts. This weeklong course is designed for medical educators, medical librarians, medical administrators, and faculty to help prepare participants to make informed decisions about computer-based tools and improve their computer skills. Topics covered during the course include database design, telemedicine, clinical decision support systems, personal health records, and much more. More information can be found at courses.mbl.edu/mi. Another helpful resource is the MLA DocKit #11 (a DocKit is a collection of representative and unedited documents from a variety of libraries), *Informatics in Health Sciences Curricula*. Published in 2005, this work includes descriptions, syllabi, assignments, and the like for informatics courses in the health sciences. MLA also has a Medical Informatics Section (www.medinfo.mlanet.org).

Informatics is an excellent target for librarians to focus on as a way to gain inroads into potential stakeholders. Librarians are in a unique position to understand and contribute to informatics, both broadly and specifically—especially librarians who really like technology. Informatics and health/medical informatics programs are springing up on a variety of campuses. If this interests you, and you need a second master's for promotion and/or tenure—or just want one—be sure and take a look at informatics programs. If you aren't in the market for another degree, lots of places also offer certificates.

Health Insurance Portability and Accountability Act

Depending on the kind of health sciences library you find yourself in, you may hear either a great deal or just passing remarks about HIPAA, the Health Insurance Portability and Accountability Act of

1996. The goal of the act was to "make sure people can take their health insurance with them when they move from one job to another" and save the healthcare industry potentially billions of dollars and increase efficiency by providing for the electronic exchange of data.[16] HIPAA consists of two parts: Title I: Health Care Access, Portability, and Renewability, and Title II: Preventing Health Care Fraud and Abuse, Administrative Simplification; Medical Reform. The part people tend to hear the most about is the Privacy Rule in Title II.

Taking effect on April 14, 2003, the Privacy Rule "provides federal protections for personal health information held by covered entities and gives patients an array of rights with respect to that information. At the same time, the Privacy Rule is balanced so that it permits the disclosure of personal health information needed for patient care and other important purposes."[17] The Privacy Rule provides for regulations for the use and disclosure of Protected Health Information, defined as; "information about a patient's past, present, or future medical treatment that contains data that can reasonably identify the patient," including payment information.[18]

Health sciences librarians, especially those working in hospital settings or with clinicians, should be prepared to familiarize themselves with HIPAA in general and the Privacy Rule specifically. Hospital librarians dealing with and serving physicians will want to make sure to help users follow HIPAA guidelines. This may mean, for instance, restricting the saving of documents to library PCs so that patient information cannot be accidentally or intentionally saved to the shared PCs in the hospital library. Working with clinicians is another area in which a good working knowledge of HIPAA will be necessary.

The jury is still out on the impact that HIPAA restrictions have on medical research. For instance, a University of Michigan study compared patient information from pre- and post-HIPAA time frames and found that following up with patients dropped from a 96.4 percent success rate pre-HIPAA to 34 percent after HIPAA.[19] Luckily, librarians have a number of good resources to choose from. If you work in an environment like a hospital library, where HIPAA is an issue, there should be plenty of in-house training opportunities. Be sure to ask your employer about those. For more information about HIPAA, visit the U.S. Department of Health and Human Services' Health Information Privacy website (www.hhs. gov/ocr/privacy).

Outreach and Marketing

Roles for health sciences librarians are constantly evolving as librarians strive to be where their users are, both physically and virtually. No longer do librarians sit at the reference desk waiting for patrons to come to them with a question or to check out a book. In health sciences environments, librarians are shifting from focusing on collections to facilitating use and access in an electronic world. While users are still coming into the physical library, many more are in their classrooms, offices, laboratories, and patient rooms. How, then, can librarians get to the users?

Remember that clinicians, researchers, and students often have really strict schedules and can't just walk over to the library whenever they feel like it. So creating "help" that is 24/7 can be an important way to reach out and provide a useful service. Think about introducing podcasts or web-based tutorials, for example, that users can access at any time instead of providing traditional, face-to-face instruction. Consider creating a pathfinder of subject-specific resources and places for patrons to start when doing research. Online pathfinders can be used to focus on specific assignments and projects or to promote the databases, journals, and resources that are pertinent to particular groups. These sorts of activities allow the library to create customized resources for particular user groups that better meet their needs and save them time. Consider holding "office hours" in other departments or schools. In other words, find a way to go to them instead of making them come to you.

Find ways to support faculty and contribute to curriculum development. Collaborate with schools in the health sciences to conduct a "mini medical school." Attend institutional animal testing committee meetings and meetings of research groups on campus. The key here, though, is not to crash the meeting. Never just show up unannounced, but use your contacts and take advantage as opportunities present themselves to say that you would love to do a 5- to 10-minute demo of a relevant resource for a committee or group. In many cases, you will become a regular, and the 5-minute demo will evolve into much longer presentations. Be sure to take advantage of whatever events your parent institution is having.

Hosting activities and programs (free food is always a good draw) during National Library Week and National Medical Librarians Month is another way to draw attention to the library. Highlight library resources during national health observances. For instance, May is Healthy Vision Month, so you could highlight the library's eye and vision resources. When a health topic is discussed in the news, such as swine flu or SARS, take the opportunity to provide reliable health information and resources on the issue.

If your institution produces newsletters, ask if you can submit something for inclusion. And don't underestimate the power of flyers, cards, and custom bookmarks. Just as pharmaceutical representatives do, deliver promotional items about the library to departments, units, and schools. Form partnerships with local public and academic libraries, and participate in area health and wellness fairs. One of the best places to gather ideas is Library Success: A Best Practices Wiki (www.libsuccess.org), which

My mother was a health sciences librarian, so I grew up hearing all the library lingo: periodicals, stacks, LC, Southern Chapter, MLA—which I knew as the Medical Library Association, not the Modern Language Association. I also saw how much my mom loved her job and the satisfaction she got from it. I was not initially drawn to librarianship; I wanted to blaze my own career path. I explored several other careers—occupational therapy, dietetics, social work, nonprofit work—but after receiving a bachelor's degree in sociology and a master's degree in public administration, I realized I did not want to limit myself to just one of these areas. I wanted to check the box next to "all of the above!" A soul-searching inventory of my interests and strengths ensued. I had a passion for health-related subjects, helping others, technology, and constantly learning new things; I also was detail-oriented, a good listener, and persistent. I wanted job security and a profession that would allow me much flexibility through the years. I soon realized that medical librarianship fit the bill!

Since completing my MLIS degree at the University of Alabama in 2001, I have had the opportunity to work in three very different library environments: an academic health sciences library serving primarily medical school and health professions students and faculty, a public health "information center" serving scientists and employees of a large federal agency, and a general academic library serving university students and faculty from a very broad range of disciplines. Each setting has its own advantages and challenges.

At the health sciences library, I benefited from being on a team of medical librarians. If I wasn't sure about the best source for a given health topic, I had many other health sciences librarians to whom I could turn for assistance. The federal agency library also had its positive aspects. I enjoyed assisting some of the top public health researchers in the world, and I found it extremely satisfying to know that they would use the information and skills I imparted to them to improve public well-being. When Hurricane Katrina hit, we librarians were called on to quickly gather key pieces of literature to support public health workers on the front lines. I was always very aware that I was employed in a federal library: I learned about contractor–federal employee interaction policies, I found myself developing a whole new vocabulary based on government acronyms, and I adhered to the strict security policies of the agency. At both the health sciences and public health agency libraries, I was surrounded by both seasoned and burgeoning health sciences librarians. These colleagues were instrumental in helping me to hone my medical reference skills.

I am currently working in a large, general academic library as a health and education "liaison librarian." I am part of a team of 16 liaison librarians, each of whom has her own areas of specialization. At my institution, liaison librarians are responsible for reference desk duty, instruction, outreach to academic departments, and collection development within their assigned areas. I have benefited tremendously from working with other nonmedical subject specialist librarians. My awareness of non–health-related resources has increased greatly, and this knowledge enables me to assist clients in a broader range of topics. As the lines between disciplines become increasingly blurred, I believe aspiring medical librarians should seek exposure to non–health-sciences library settings as well.

Susan Smith is Liaison Librarian for Nutrition, Physical Therapy, Respiratory Therapy, Kinesiology and Health, and Early Childhood Education at Georgia State University Library (www.library.gsu.edu) in Atlanta, Georgia.

compiles information on "successful programs and ... innovative things with technology that no one outside [the] library knows about." This wiki covers ideas and examples of projects on all sorts of topics, including management and leadership, reference service and information literacy, selling your library (marketing and promotion), technology, and training and development.

Remember to keep in mind that outreach and marketing go hand in hand. So make sure that, whatever you do in terms of outreach, you aren't breaking any rules or crossing any cultural taboos within your institution. You don't want bad press. And don't spam people; make sure the communications you produce are targeted to each specific group. If you send a broad, general email about library resources to the whole university or hospital, it will just end up being deleted. Effective marketing is about promoting a specific resource to a specific group, preferably right at the time it is needed. It is as simple as promoting study rooms at exam time—but to the students, not the faculty. Another key is finding out how particular groups like to get their news. For instance, some schools may have an actual physical bulletin board for important announcements because students don't get to check their email until they get home. Ask if you can put library information there.

Successful outreach and marketing are about knowing your assets and your users.

Another important component is your brand. You need a logo or graphic element of some kind, even if it is just the library name in the same font, on every single thing you produce. Think about what athletic departments do. They have a logo, a mascot, colors, and so forth, which all elicit powerful responses from fans. While this may be an extreme example, it is also a good one: Marketing and branding are about creating loyal fans. Branding is about getting into users' hearts and minds. You want people to associate that brand with the library (hopefully, in a good way). Think for a minute—do you have a favorite brand of anything? Are there logos that you immediately associate with quality and dependability? On the other hand, are there companies you will not buy from? When you see their logo, how do you feel? When folks see a library publication, whether it's print or electronic, how do you want them to feel? Don't just limit yourself to library literature and resources in outreach and marketing. Often, resources from other fields can be helpful as well.

While none of these activities are "one size fits all," they should provide some examples and food for thought. Many of the respondents to our survey emphasized how important outreach and marketing are for libraries. When asked what they see as the greatest challenge for health sciences libraries, participants mentioned:

- "Keeping abreast of new methods of delivering services."

- "Marketing—getting the word out that you exist."

- "Reaching out to patrons where they are—beyond the library. And marketing what we do even as we try to appear seamless."

- "Look for out-of-the-box ways we [can] bring our skills and expertise to the table."

Ultimately, no matter what sort of library you work in, the most important thing is to figure out what will work for your specific library and population and make sure that whatever you produce has your library's logo or at least your library's name. Not only does this work toward creating your brand, but it also serves to let folks know that resource X is provided by the library. A word of warning: It is easy to get carried away with marketing and outreach. It is fun and addictive. Don't try to do too much all at once; start small, and build slowly.

Endnotes

1. Michelle L. Eberle, "Librarians' Perceptions of the Reference Interview," *Journal of Hospital Librarianship* 5, no. 3 (2005): 35.

2. Quick Guide to Health Literacy, Fact Sheet, "Health Literacy Basics," www.health.gov/communication/literacy/quickguide/factsbasic.htm

3. Medical Library Association, "Consumer Health Information Specialization Policies and Procedures," www.mlanet.org/pdf/ce/chis_p&p_06.pdf

4. Frank Davidoff and Valerie Florance, "The Informationist: A New Health Profession?" *Annals of Internal Medicine* 132, no. 12 (June 2000): 996.

5. Association of Academic Health Sciences Libraries, "Building on Success: Charting the Future of Knowledge Management Within the Academic Health Center," AAHSL Charting the Future Task Force, 2003, data.memberclicks.com/site/aahsl/Building-On-Success.pdf

6. Nunzia B. Guise, Taneya Y. Koonce, Rebecca N. Jerome, Molynda Cahall, Nila A. Sathe, and Annette Williams, "Evolution of a Mature Clinical Informationist Model," *Journal of the American Medical Informatics Association* 12, no. 3 (May/June 2005): 250.

7. Ibid.

8. Centre for Evidence Based Medicine, "What Is EBM?" www.cebm.net/ebm_is_isnt.asp

9. Cleo Pappas, "Evidence-Based Medicine: An Overview and Teaching Tips," *Journal of Hospital Librarianship* 8, no. 1 (2008): 1–15.

10. Susan W. Salmond, "Advancing Evidence-Based Practice: A Primer," *Orthopaedic Nursing* 26, no. 2 (Mar./Apr. 2007): 114–123.

11. Cynthia D. Mulrow, Deborah J. Cook, and Frank Davidoff, "Systematic Reviews: Critical Links in the Great Chain of Evidence," *Annals of Internal Medicine* 126, no. 5 (Mar. 1997): 389–391.

12. Deborah J. Cook, Cynthia D. Mulrow, and R. Brian Haynes, "Systematic Reviews: Synthesis of Best Evidence for Clinical Decisions," *Annals of Internal Medicine* 126, no. 5 (Mar. 1997): 378.

13. Jessie McGowan and Margaret Sampson, "Systematic Reviews Need Systematic Searchers," *Journal of the Medical Library Association* 93, no. 1 (Jan. 2005): 76.

14. National Institutes of Health Public Access, "NIH Public Access Policy Details," publicaccess.nih.gov/policy.htm

15. American Medical Informatics Association, "About AMIA," www.amia.org/inside

16. Kathy Rockel, *Stedman's Guide to the HIPAA Privacy Rule* (Philadelphia: Lippincott Williams & Wilkins, 2006), 2.

17. U.S. Department of Health and Human Services, "Understanding HIPAA Privacy," www.hhs.gov/ocr/privacy/hipaa/understanding

18. Rockel, *Stedman's Guide*, 9.

19. David Armstrong, Eva Kline-Rogers, Sandeep M. Jani, Edward B. Goldman, Jianming Fang, Debabrata Mukherjee, Brahmajee K. Nallamothu, and Kim A. Eagle. "Potential Impact of the HIPAA Privacy Rule on Data Collection in a Registry of Patients with Acute Coronary Syndrome," *Archives of Internal Medicine* 165, no. 10 (May 2005): 1125–1129.

Chapter 4

Technology

Technology ... is a queer thing. It brings you great gifts with one hand, and it stabs you in the back with the other.

—C. P. Snow

Technology is an integral part of any library setting, and all librarians should expect technology to be a driving force in their work life—and to take up a substantial part of their continuing education efforts. When asked "What are the greatest challenges in health sciences librarianship today?" many respondents mentioned issues with technology. Whether in terms of dealing with information technology (IT) outfits, providing access, keeping up, teaching users about technology, or proving librarians' worth in the internet age, technology is on everyone's mind. Technology's impact is apparent in survey responses like these:

- "Navigating changes in publishing—online versus print, access, authority, cost, and the perception that librarians aren't necessary with everything 'free on the web.'"

- "New technological innovations ... almost something new on a daily basis."

- "Being able to keep up with the constant changes in technology."

- "Ever-changing technology impacting on our role."

- "Vendors constantly changing/upgrading the tools/interfaces especially without sufficient beta testing. It's all supposed to be new and better (see how shiny it is?!!) but performance fails. Vendors don't seem to understand the need for simplicity, efficiency, reliability, and cost control."

- "Fixing the photocopier and troubleshooting basic computer issues."

- "The problem of being in this academic library is that we've had a director who follows the corporate model, is only interested in technology, and does not value the health sciences."

- "Technology has fooled administration into thinking we need fewer resources and fewer staff."

Whether they love technology or hate it, librarians are no strangers to technostress. The technology-related comments received on our brief survey are eerily similar to the comments received back in 1996 on a survey for the thesis, "Technostress in the Reference Environment: A Survey of U.S. Association of Research Libraries Academic Reference Librarians."[1] When discussing the role of a technology manager, authors Ruth Holst and Sharon A. Phillips point out that "keeping current with rapidly changing computing hardware, software, and networking capabilities requires an understanding of computing and technology concepts and skillful management of technological change." They go on to say that "a knowledge of computing technology is clearly fundamental ... [and] librarians need to know how computers work and how they can be connected and configured to provide appropriate levels of user access."[2]

Health sciences librarians require no specific technical skills outside the general skills *all* librarians need. However, the health sciences fields are pushed and pulled by technology, creating an environment where library stakeholders expect the best and newest technology available. People needing health information, especially clinicians, want that information right now, they want it electronically, and they want it delivered directly to a digital device (desktop, phone, or PDA).

Those that have stumbled into being a health sciences librarian may find the technology demands overwhelming. No one list of technology-related skills fits every accidental health sciences librarian, because too much depends on specific circumstances and environments. Hospital librarians face different technological demands and challenges than academic health sciences librarians, for example. Health sciences librarians can, however, do a few things to increase their ability to successfully deal with technology, and just having a basic understanding of certain technologies will help immensely. It comes down to this: The more you know, the more effective you can be. You don't need to be an engineer or really even have an inherent aptitude for technology. Just work on developing a nice set of core competencies and a powerful IT vocabulary that will allow you to communicate better with the technology folks you encounter. All you need is determination.

Communicating With IT

No matter what kind of health sciences library you find yourself in, you'll need to communicate with an array of people about technology. These range from vendor support to a desktop technician, a network engineer, or your institution's chief information officer, and your ability to effectively communicate with these people will greatly increase your ability to get things done—and significantly lower your frustration level.

One of the best ways to improve communication with IT is to learn their language. Every profession has its own jargon, and just taking the time to call things by the correct name will go a long way toward getting your issue resolved. Start with a couple of good basic reference resources on PCs and networking, keep them close at hand, and think about taking a course on basic technology topics (or those specific to your institution). Realize, though, that taking a course takes time (and usually money). You may, understandably, encounter some push back when you suggest taking a course. Librarians' own excuses for not keeping up with technology run the gamut from "I don't have time" to "I'll never use that" and all the way to "It isn't my job to understand the technology." The rewards, however, of making the time to take a class—even if you never use the course material for its original purpose—far outweigh the negatives. For suggestions on specific technologies to learn, see the "Keeping Up" section later in this chapter.

Any time you take a technology-oriented course, you open yourself up to a new vocabulary and new ideas, and gain experience with technology in the broader sense. That alone is worth its weight in gold. After a few courses, you will find that you are starting to think more like the IT guys, navigate your own computer better, and, hopefully, make some new contacts. Start out with something fun like a digital photography class (which might even be offered at your local public library). Don't worry too much about it being directly work-related; any exposure to different technologies and different kinds of technology geeks is beneficial. And, as a side note, it also makes you more marketable.

If money is an issue, you can find more and more free opportunities for technology training. First, check to see if your institution offers free training. Check with local colleges and universities to see what sort of continuing education training they offer. Schools often offer training at a much lower price than computer learning centers do. Also check in your local area for technology-related user groups and associations. For instance, the Internet Professionals Society of Alabama (ipsaonline.org) offers a free monthly lunch event, while user groups are generally free or very cheap and hold regular meetings as well as special events. Don't forget to check out the public library in your area as well; it may offer free computer classes on a variety of topics.

If you're interested in self-study, also look for free online tutorials and user forums on specific technology topics. You could even try developing a monthly class for library staff—invite the people from IT to come or even to teach. It may take a few tries, but your persistence will eventually pay off. If your own IT people are too busy, ask someone from a local college or university to come talk about topics such as how wireless works. Another good option for technology training is your local community college; these institutions often offer a nice array of courses.

Computer learning centers are also an option, but since they generally focus on helping IT professionals get certified, they tend to be pricier and tend to gear their material to optimizing students' chances of passing the certification test. There are, however, two certifications that may be beneficial for accidental health sciences librarians. CompTIA's A+ and Network+ certifications are entry-level certifications for PC and network technicians. Taken together, they provide a really strong foundation and would definitely give any librarian a boost when dealing with IT outfits. If you are interested in these certifications, just drop by your local bookstore or public library and look for some study guides to see what types of topics they cover. Or you may just want to invest in one of these study guides for use as a quick reference manual. Just be forewarned: Getting certifications can become addictive (and expensive).

Dealing with and learning about technology can be very overwhelming. There are tons of areas you *could* investigate—but what *should* you investigate? No one can be an expert in everything, so take a look around and see what areas of expertise seem to be missing or what technological problem areas your library experiences. If you are doing well with the guys that support your desktop PCs but never can get through to the networking guys, try brushing up on networking. If you are having trouble getting through to the web guys, then brush up on that area. Start small and grow from there, but always focus on developing good communication and relationships with your IT department(s).

The more you know, the better you can explain to your IT people what is needed, the better you'll be able to understand the IT guys, and the better you'll be able to handle situations with patrons when the technology isn't behaving. The more you know, the more efficiently you'll be able to get things accomplished. Talking like a techie will get you noticed and heard. Hospital librarians in particular often don't have direct access to any of the technology they use and are behind a firewall that prevents various forms of access. In this situation, you will have to go through your IT department for everything, even just posting a webpage—making that communication and those relationships even more critical.

Managing Your Expectations and Attitude

If you follow the advice to keep technologically up to date, then managing your attitude and expectations about technology will come more easily. In other words, the more you know about the technology used in your environment, the better prepared you will be when that technology behaves in an unexpected way—or fails completely. Today's libraries interact with and contain various complex information and communication systems. If just one piece of a system is misbehaving, this can cause unexpected behaviors throughout the entire infrastructure. This goes for desktop PCs, as well. If any of your PC's hardware or software is experiencing a problem, then your PC may exhibit odd behavior in a variety of ways. You should expect your technology to work, but you should also expect to have issues from time to time. Knowing some good basic troubleshooting tips and making a cheat sheet of resolutions to common problems will help a great deal.

Remember that technology works on a very specific set of instructions. We aren't yet to the point where everyday technology can infer what we mean; it only knows what data it has received. Along the same lines, technologies are designed to do certain things—and sometimes those aren't the certain things we want these technologies to do. When you are looking to purchase new equipment or software, it's important that you know what you want the technology to do and exactly what the technology you are buying does. You want the right tool for the job, so you need to know what the job is, as well as what the available tools are.

It is great when technology works the way it should and the way it's expected to. When it doesn't, though, it's both easy and tempting to blame the vendor and the support people. Avoid this trap if at all possible; avoid taking out your frustration with the technology on people. While it may sometimes feel as if librarians and IT people are opponents rather than partners, do your best to avoid contributing to this attitude. Rudeness will get you nowhere, so wait until you get home to rant. Remember that technology isn't perfect, that there will be days when it fails, and that the IT people get just as frustrated with the technology as you do. Here, again, making an effort to learn all you can about the technology where you work will help you be better able to keep things in perspective.

Another useful lesson in dealing with IT is this: When you have a need, don't tell the IT folks what you *need*. Instead, tell them what you are trying to *do*. In other words, don't give them the solution, give them the problem. Instead of saying "I need a hole in our hospital firewall," try saying "We need to provide access to this important commercial resource the hospital just paid a ton of money to acquire for our physicians providing primary care in rural areas. How can we best accomplish this?" Like librarians, IT people love problem solving.

Accidental librarian does describe me, not only from the health sciences perspective, but in terms of librarianship in general. But sometimes, accidents are the greatest things that happen.

I graduated from college in 1987 with a business major. As with most new graduates, I was full of ideas and thought that I would change business dealings as we knew them. Au contraire, mon frère. Practicing bankers and others that I interviewed with felt that I should start in a boring position and make little money until "I was ready" to do "more important" things. And, while I did not mind paying my dues, I was bored out of my mind. So I was always looking around me for new opportunities. At the time, a friend of mine was working in a small academic library. She moved into a new position and her job became open. She told me that she thought that I should apply for the job. I did and got it! I fell in love with working with people in the information provision field.

After about a year at this job, I began working on my MLS. I truly loved the experience of those classes. Again, I learned a great deal—but this time had the perspective of actually working while studying, so I was a little more prepared for the "real world" of librarianship as compared to my undergrad degree fantasies. When I finished my MLS, I began to search for a professional job. Luckily for me, a hospital at the time was looking for a librarian to work with its family practice residency program. What a break for me! I found my calling. I had a great relationship with my doctors and residents and appreciated everything they taught me. I was a one-person library and responsible for all aspects of library service.

I worked at that job for five years and then moved to a larger hospital. Unfortunately for me, that particular hospital was sold to a larger for-profit group and then closed. So once again, I was in search of a job. I moved to take a job as the director of a small public library system, but oh, how I missed my health sciences environment. I was lucky that a job became available at Lister Hill Library at the University of Alabama at Birmingham. I interviewed for and accepted that job. I worked at Lister Hill for two years and then moved into my current role as a serials vendor librarian. My true love is still active librarianship within a health sciences library. So beware I may show up in your library!

Jodi Kuehl is an Account Services Manager for EBSCO Information Services (www.ebsco.com) in Birmingham, Alabama.

Keeping Up

Don't even try. Yes, that's right; we're telling you to not even try to keep up with Technology (with a capital T). You can't, no one can, and you'll only frustrate yourself and wreck your home life if you try. Now, if Technology is your thing, then by all means go for it— but for most librarians, dealing with how the technology works isn't what they "do" every day. Librarians, however, do *use* technology every day. Your goal should be to become a "power user." Make the effort to use technology to its fullest and to be able to advocate for your library and your library users where technology is concerned.

So, where do you start? If nothing jumps out at you as a problem area, then start with what is right in front of you.

Your PC

Your PC is your best friend and your worst enemy. It helps you work; it distracts you from work; it does wondrous things; it does nothing you need it to do. In short, if you are looking for a place to start gaining a techie's knowledge and vocabulary you'll be best off starting with the humming box on (or under) your desk. Just gaining a general knowledge of what is inside a PC and how it makes software "go" can vastly improve the relationship between you and your computer. Like any machine, PCs need love and attention. They need to be kept clean—both figuratively and literally. They need to have software installed responsibly. They need to have the right hardware. If you've never looked inside a PC, grab a screwdriver and do it! If and when you upgrade your home system, keep the old one to tear up. And, by all means, get a generic PC reference book such as Scott Mueller's *Upgrading and Repairing PCs* (now in its 18th edition from Que Press). Another great place to start is on the HowStuffWorks website (computer.howstuffworks.com). HowStuffWorks contains easy-to-read illustrated articles as well as a number of videos. Of course, you can Google just about anything tech related and get more information than you would ever need.

Your Network and Remote Access Methods

Perhaps one of the most complex and most "issue" prone areas is that of networking and remote access. There are so many components, variables, and people involved that diagnosing network issues can be a long, frustrating experience rife with trial and error. Often librarians find themselves smack in the middle as their database vendors and their organization's network department each blame the other for the failure. To further aggravate matters, when the network is down, not much is available. You can't just move users to another network the way you can move them to another machine if a specific PC crashes. Here again, basic troubleshooting skills and a powerful vocabulary can be your best friends. When you begin learning about technology, be sure to learn how a basic network functions, and then learn as much as you can about your organization's network and who runs it. When there is a problem, be prepared to help diagnose the issue—because the problem could be anything from a local PC's network card going bad to a power outage with a major provider in an entirely different city.

For instance, if you get a call telling you that the "internet is down," work your way out from the problem. First, know who to call to see if they already know what is going on. Second, check to see if you can get to a site from another PC. If you can, then it may just be that a particular PC has lost its connection. Rebooting will probably fix the issue. Or check the network cable: Is it plugged in, are the little lights by the cable plug on the PC on, is the wire crimped or cracked? (If so, replace it!) Third, see if you can access sites within your own domain. In other words, can you get to other sites that your organization maintains? In a university library scenario, for instance, you might try accessing the school of nursing website. If you can get to your own organization's sites but not to other sites, like Google, then that tells you that the issue is most likely somewhere outside your organization. Your IT or networking department will need to contact the outside provider. (Of course, the same is true if you can't get to anything, even to internal sites.)

On the other hand, if you can get to Google, but not to any of your own sites, then your web server may have crashed. Luckily for librarians, these issues tend to be handled quickly—because if you can't get to your email or website, neither can the CEO or president. Other issues, like remote access issues, are not so easily resolved. These usually revolve around three things: a firewall, proxy servers with unique user names and passwords, and virtual private networks (VPNs). See the next few sections for more information on each of these topics.

Firewalls

Network administrators' honor and worth is tied to their network's stability and security. What keeps us all secure? The network firewall. HowStuffWorks.com describes a firewall as "a barrier to keep destructive forces away from your property," while Wikipedia defines it as "a dedicated appliance, or software running on another computer, which inspects network traffic passing through it, and denies or permits passage based on a set of rules."[3] As long as you are warm and cozy within the firewall (on campus or inside your hospital, for example), then all is well. When you travel outside your home institution's firewall, however (say, to clinics in rural towns), or when you put yourself behind the firewall of another entity (such as a Veterans' Affairs [VA] hospital or pharmaceutical research facility), reaching the resources that were once right at your fingertips becomes immensely more challenging.

Here's one common scenario: A doctor attached to your organization has accepted an additional appointment at the local VA hospital. This VA hospital has provided him with an office and new PC. The doctor would love to use his new office but finds he can no longer access any of your library's resources. He calls you, the health sciences librarian, and reports the problem. The first thing you should ask this physician (and anyone with a similar issue) is "Where are you?" If he says he is in a health or research facility not affiliated with your library's organization, it is pretty safe to assume he is behind a firewall. But, now that you know what a firewall is, you can explain to that physician what is going on. He or you will have to connect with the IT department of that other organization so that it can enable access to your library's resources.

Note that, as outlined in the Wikipedia definition, traffic is allowed to pass or enter through a firewall based on certain rules. Those rules can be configured to allow traffic from or to specific resources like a proxy server or database. Remember, however, that

those network administrators are charged with keeping the network and data safe. They'll need to document any requests carefully and get all their t's crossed and i's dotted—in case something
terrible happens and someone important asks why there was a
hole in the firewall that allowed a virus in that corrupted all their
financial data. So be persistent, but be patient.

Proxy Servers and User Names and Passwords

When most libraries subscribe to electronic resources they do so
with the understanding that their population should be able to
access those resources no matter where they are (firewall issues
notwithstanding). Therefore, they need some method of authenti-
cating users. In essence, something has to ask users who they are,
then check to see if they do indeed have access to the resource.
Health sciences libraries most commonly use a unique login for
each user or a combination of a login and proxy server.

When a subscription is initially set up, the library provides its
vendor with a range of IP addresses. These IP addresses are added
to the vendor's (yep, you guessed it!) firewall. Now, when someone
accesses that resource from within the library, hospital, or school,
the firewall looks for the IP address of the machine requesting
access. If the IP of the requesting machine is in the range of allowed
IPs, access is granted. If not, the user must be authenticated in
another way before access is granted. In some cases users can create an account from a machine within the specified IP range, then
use their user name and password to access that resource from a
remote location. This method, however, is cumbersome. It requires
users to come to your location, which is not always possible, and
requires vendors to house and store a number of random user
names that could still be used after someone has moved on.

Enter the proxy server. While there are many types of proxy
servers, they can broadly be defined as "a server (a computer system or an application program) that services the requests of its

clients [the user and PC] by forwarding requests to other servers. A client connects to the proxy server, requesting some service, such as a file, connection, webpage, or other resource, available from a different server. The proxy server provides the resource by connecting to the specified server and requesting the service on behalf of the client."[4] One of the most popular proxy servers for libraries, installed in more than 2,500 institutions in more than 60 countries, is EZproxy (www.oclc.org/ezproxy).[5] EZproxy is a web proxy program that allows people access to library resources from, potentially, anywhere.

EZproxy users embed a "snippet" (such as http://www.lhl.uab.edu/8c/8.cgi?) at the beginning of the URL for a given resource, which makes the user go through the proxy server before being taken to the actual resource. So, for instance, a URL to PubMed that goes through a proxy server would look something like this: http://www.lhl.uab.edu/8c/8.cgi?http://www.ncbi.nlm.nih.gov. When an EZproxy link is selected, the user actually goes to the proxy server first. The proxy server asks: Are you within my IP range? If so, then the user proceeds automatically to PubMed. If not, then the user has to tell EZproxy who she is. EZproxy prompts the user for a user name and password. If the user name and password (usually assigned by the school or institution) are in the proxy server, then the user is passed on to PubMed. If not, she gets an access denied message. This solution allows libraries to maintain user names and passwords on their end, allowing them to remove folks who move on to other jobs or graduate from the user file as needed.

Most of the issues with EZproxy (or any other proxy server) have to do with its configuration file. Unless you are managing the software yourself, you probably won't have access to that file. But you do have access to the configuration guide on OCLC's site at www.oclc.org/support/documentation/ezproxy/db/default.htm, as well as to an RSS feed that announces "recent additions and changes to database specific configuration instructions."[6] If some-one is having trouble with an EZproxy login, try to get a screenshot of whatever is happening, take a look at the configuration guide, check whether there are any updates, and send all of the informa-tion to the person who manages your EZproxy. Gathering the background information will only take about five minutes but will get you a much faster result. If you use some method of authenti-cation other than EZproxy, familiarize yourself with its resources and keep that information handy as well.

Your VPN

If your organization provides access via a VPN, the VPN can often help with remote access issues. A VPN is a network "that uses the public internet as a backbone for private interconnection (net-work) between locations."[7] To use a VPN, you most often will need to install a little piece of software on your PC to use when you are in a remote location. When you initiate the VPN software, you log in with a user name and password that allow you to enter a space on the internet that looks and behaves exactly as if you were at work or school. In most cases you won't be managing a VPN directly—there are luckily some very smart network administra-tors who make it work. But if you have access to a VPN, it is an easy-to-use and powerful tool to recommend to your library's users.

No one is suggesting you have to learn all this information on your first week on the job. In fact, much of this you'll end up assim-ilating on the job as you use the technology every day. If you pay attention and keep a running list of troubleshooting tips, you'll end up knowing a lot more than you think—and in a very short time. Put a little effort into learning about the technology that is in your immediate surroundings, and you will be amazed at what you can do and how much it can help you do your job.

The Web and Social Networking

All too often librarians are at the mercy of those who control their web server, since so much depends on the software installed on and the configuration of that server. Even if you aren't creating much web content yourself, knowing how webpages work, especially how your organization's webpage works, will help you troubleshoot errors and better serve your users. In many cases, librarians are pushed by their administration to create web content but aren't allowed to post content to the live web server. This can create a frustrating environment in which librarians have to explain to their boss why something can't be made available immediately, while justifying to their web administrators why they need a given page or application posted. Here again, the more you know, the better off you are. First, know the process to get files posted to the web server, and follow this process. If you do have access to the live server, then follow any instructions very carefully. Most of us at one point or another have accidentally overwritten the wrong page or deleted the wrong thing. Ask whether the organization maintains a development server, or a testing server that isn't visible to the world at large. Ask for an account there so that you can work on web projects and test them out before they go "live."[8] Work *should* be done in a test environment, and just knowing the phrase *development server* will pique the interest of your IT folks.

If you are going to make and use web content, you'll need to know basic HTML. There are so many HTML resources on the internet that you can easily find out how to structure a basic webpage. Think you don't need to know HTML anymore because of all the ready-made social networking applications? Think again. If you want to install a Meebo (www.meebo.com) widget so you can do chat reference, could you install that code so that it appears on your page correctly? If you wanted a widget to appear on multiple pages, could you create a simple include, so that if you make modifications to that widget, those changes would appear everywhere, automatically? If you wanted to install Google Analytics (www. google.com/analytics), would you be able to? Even if you do not create the pages yourself, being able to look at a file and tell—even just generally—what is going on will be a tremendous help. And if you do start a blog or a wiki with one of those ready-made social networking applications, that little bit of HTML knowledge will help you avoid display errors and take greater advantage of those free tools.

Like many other libraries, health sciences libraries are hopping on the Web 2.0 bandwagon and trying to do more with social networking in an effort to reach users. Libraries are posting videos on YouTube, creating blogs, and setting up RSS feeds of new books or library news. Here are just a few examples to spark your own ideas:

- The Ebling Library for the Health Sciences at the University of Wisconsin–Madison has a news blog at ebling.library.wisc.edu/blog.

- Search YouTube for "health sciences library" or "medical library," and you'll find tons of videos on library services, resources, tutorials, and events. The University of Florida's Health Science Center Library, for instance, has a tour of its library available on YouTube (www.youtube.com/watch?v=Fg31F-9QJOk).

- The University of Colorado–Denver Health Sciences Library (twitter.com/UCDenverHSL) and the University of Buffalo Health Sciences Library (twitter.com/UBHSL) both use Twitter to communicate with their users about new resources, events, and the like.

- Facebook has also attracted a number of health sciences libraries, including the Health Sciences Library at the University of North Carolina at Chapel Hill (www.face book.com/pages/Chapel-Hill-NC/UNC-Health-Sciences-Library/10473632902#/pages/Chapel-Hill-NC/UNC-Health-Sciences-Library/10473632902).

Health sciences libraries are using tools such as AddThis (www.addthis.com) on their websites to allow users to easily bookmark and share library webpages or resources. The Duke University Medical Center Library has created a library search gadget (www.gmodules.com/ig/creator?synd=open&nocache=1&url=http://www.mclibrary.duke.edu/gadgets/mclgadget.xml&nocache=1) with Google Gadget that users can add to their own pages, allowing them to search the library's website, catalog, ejournals, PubMed, and DynaMed from one box. Some libraries are also finding ways to use social bookmarking tools like Delicious to deliver library content. Chattahoochee Technical College Library, for example, is using Delicious to create lists of resources for various programs such as allied health resources (delicious.com/nmtc_Librarian/bundle:AlliedHealth). Others, like the University of

Tour of the University of Florida's Health Science Center Library on YouTube

Spencer S. Eccles Health Sciences Library Facebook page

Maryland's Health Sciences and Human Services Library and the Medical College of Georgia Library, are creating podcasts and contributing to iTunes U.

The world really is wide open when it comes to using Web 2.0 applications—but that doesn't mean you should try to do it all today. These tools are only good and useful if they are maintained and relevant. When you choose a tool, make sure to continue spending time with it, promoting it, and maintaining it. See what folks are already using. If your users love Twitter but hate Facebook, don't do a Facebook page just because other libraries have one. Also keep in mind any network restrictions your institution may have in place. In many hospitals, employees can't access Facebook anyway! That doesn't necessarily mean you shouldn't have a Facebook page, but you need to evaluate the situation in terms of what you are trying to accomplish.

Whenever I tell someone that I am a librarian, one of the first things they say is "You must love to read." As any librarian knows, the love of reading does not make one a librarian. When I tell someone I am a medical librarian, I usually get a puzzled look and a response of "I never knew there were medical librarians." Well, I didn't either—until I met one.

My nursing school background seemed to put me on the path of medical librarianship. Seeing all the wonderful things I could do as a medical librarian has kept me there and propelled me into a career and a life I would never have thought possible. I would never have started on the path to librarianship, however, if not for a special person. She was also a medical librarian, but I didn't know it at the time. We met in Germany.

I had my first job as a library aide in an elementary school on a German army post. As the troops were drawing down, the school was closed, and the library director on the American post was retiring after 17 years. After almost a year of working as a library aide, I was now infinitely qualified to stand in until the new librarian came. I somehow spent the next few months figuring out how to run a library. First came weeding, literally, through 17 years of materials. As librarians, we also don't tend to throw things out! The wonderful day finally arrived, and the new librarian came. Truly, until I met her, I never knew how wonderful librarianship could be. She took me under her wing and made me use this thing called a computer. How patient she was, and what an unwilling student I was. Still she persevered, and as I saw her manage the library, I knew exactly what I wanted to do when I returned to the U.S.

She told me there were other librarians called medical librarians. She told me how she had been a medical librarian, did an internship, and learned how to search this thing called MEDLINE—and that she had had to study it for a long time. I have to thank Janice Missiledine because without her I would truly never have chosen the path of librarianship.

When I returned to the U.S., I worked in a public library, a newspaper library, and eventually became a director of a naturopathic medical college. Mind you, I had still not gotten my master's degree in library science. I couldn't wait any longer, so I went to Indiana University and finally learned what librarianship could be. Upon graduation, my first job was as lead reference and collection development librarian at Charles Drew University in Los Angeles. From here I was introduced to a new field that integrated all of my interests: health sciences informatics. I may not have librarian on my business cards anymore, but I am still a medical librarian. I retrieve, organize, and communicate information to my patrons every day. They just don't know they're patrons.

Soraya Assar, MLS, is Senior Consultant for IBM Middle East, Global Business Services (www-304.ibm.com/jct 03004c/businesscenter/smb/us/en/solutionsummary/xml id/79215).

Speaking of social networking and free software, the phrase "be where the users are" is thrown around a lot. Whether you buy into that concept, or whether you buy into Web 2.0, social software is here to stay. We aren't going to address every available type of social networking services and software. Plenty of librarians have weighed in on everything from Second Life to RSS to podcasting to Facebook. You can find wonderful case studies with lots of useful information, but your goal here is not to jump on every new whiz-bang thing that comes down the pike. Your goal is to harness the power and flexibility these tools offer *for your specific needs*. In other words, find the right tool for your needs, don't create a need to fit a tool. Another key is to think creatively about these tools. For instance, when you think of a blog, what do you think of? An online journal? That was their original purpose. But if you think of a blog as an easy way to provide users with news, resource updates, or a full-fledged newsletter, suddenly blog software becomes an easy way to provide information to users. Try to think in terms of what the software does, not what it was originally intended for. When you're contemplating using any of these free social software tools, it's again important to know your network. For example, if you work in a university setting, you can easily set up a free blog hosted outside the university, and your users can access it with ease. But if you are in a hospital setting, your users may not be able to get to anything that isn't installed on one of the hospital's servers.

There really isn't a right or wrong place to start; the main thing is that you start building your IT knowledge and vocabulary. Health sciences librarians are bombarded with technology from both the library field and the health sciences field. Whether you are a solo librarian in a hospital or research center, or part of a large academic institution, the more time you spend with technology, the more comfortable you will be with technology. The better IT vocabulary you have, the better off you will be.

Endnotes

1. Lisa A. Ennis, "Technostress in the Reference Environment: A Survey of U.S. Association of Research Libraries Academic Reference Librarians" (MS thesis, University of Tennessee Knoxville, 1998).

2. Ruth Holst and Sharon A. Phillips, "Administrative Issues," in *The Medical Library Association Guide to Managing Health Care Libraries*, ed. Ruth Holst and Sharon A. Phillips (New York: Neal-Schuman, 2000), 26.

3. HowStuffWorks, "How Firewalls Work," computer.howstuffworks.com/firewall.htm, and Wikipedia, "Firewall," en.wikipedia.org/wiki/Firewall

4. Wikipedia, "Proxy Server," en.wikipedia.org/wiki/Proxy_server. There are also a number of different kinds of proxy servers listed on the Wikipedia site.

5. OCLC, "EZproxy Authentication and Access Software at a Glance," www.oclc.org/us/en/ezproxy/about/default.htm. Incidentally, EZproxy was written and developed by a librarian, Chris Zagar of Estrella Mountain Community College.

6. OCLC, "EZproxy Feeds," www.oclc.org/ezproxy/support/feeds.htm

7. David Groth, *Network+ Study Guide* (Sybex, 2005), 488.

8. For the bold, any PC can be turned into a web server. Apache (www.apache.org), PHP (www.php.net), and MySQL (www.mysql.com) are all free downloadable programs. The configuration can be tricky, but as always, there are numerous free tutorials all over the web.

Chapter 5

Databases and Resources

Knowledge is of two kinds. We know a subject our-
selves, or we know where we can find information
on it.

—Samuel Johnson

Given the hundreds of thousands of health sciences related
resources available to librarians, clinicians, and consumers, this
chapter doesn't contain a complete list of resources by any stretch
of the imagination. Here, we'll simply highlight some of the most
popular and important resources that accidental health sciences
librarians may encounter. Accidental health sciences librarians in
general academic or public libraries, though, should realize that
their institution won't likely have access to most of these resources.
They will either be too esoteric (like NORD) or too expensive (like
many!). However, just knowing that these resources exist can help
you make referrals to other health sciences librarians whose
libraries may have access to the necessary resource. After all, the
best resource is always another librarian.

Article and Citation Databases

PubMed and MEDLINE

Today, most people use PubMed and MEDLINE interchangeably.
However, these are actually two separate entities. MEDLINE is
actually the primary component of PubMed (www.pubmed.gov),
which is part of the Entrez databases developed by the National
Library of Medicine (NLM) National Center for Biotechnology

Information (NCBI). MEDLINE (through PubMed) is probably the go-to database for most health sciences librarians.

MEDLINE is the NLM's premier bibliographic database for biomedical and health sciences journal articles. MEDLINE, which stands for MEDLARS Online, is an outgrowth of MED-LARS (Medical Literature Analysis and Retrieval System). MED-LARS began in 1957 as the Index Mechanization Project to automate the process of compiling the *Index Medicus* and the annual *Cumulated Index Medicus*. At that time, if you wanted to use MEDLARS to perform a literature search, a trained MED-LARS search specialist would have to complete the search for you. Researchers had to fill out a MEDLARS search form and mail it to NLM, where a typist would convert the search to machine-readable form. The search would be performed, and the results sent back in the mail. The turnaround time for this entire process was several weeks.

After MEDLARS was launched in 1964, NLM began to duplicate the MEDLARS tapes for medical school libraries around the country. The first regional MEDLARS center opened at the University of Colorado in 1965. In 1966, MEDLARS centers opened at the University of Alabama, the University of Michigan, and Harvard University. This created an increased demand for MEDLARS searches, and users began to expect a two-day turnaround. Only about 20,000 requests could be fulfilled in a year, though, so NLM was unable to keep up with the number of requests for searches. Work on MEDLINE began in 1969, and the system was implemented in 1971. MEDLINE was received keenly by the medical and health sciences community. By 1987, more than 3 million searches were performed each year.

Today MEDLINE contains more than 18 million citations and abstracts and covers the fields of medicine, dentistry, nursing, veterinary medicine, the healthcare system, and preclinical sciences. MEDLINE covers topics ranging from pharmacology to diseases to psychology and includes citations from more than 5,000 journals in 37 different languages. The database covers material from the 1950s to the present and is updated almost every day. A search of MEDLINE retrieves a list of citations—author, title, publication, and sometimes an abstract; you can search MEDLINE for no charge through PubMed. Commercial organizations, such as Ovid, Dialog, and EBSCO, also lease MEDLINE from the NLM and offer access to it for a fee.

PubMed, released in 1997, provides free access to MEDLINE. Citations in PubMed are assigned a number known as the PMID (PubMed Unique Identifier). While MEDLINE contains only citations, PubMed provides links to some full-text articles. In addition to MEDLINE citations, PubMed incorporates approximately 1.8 million OLDMEDLINE citations. OLDMEDLINE citations were

PubMed homepage

originally available in printed indexes from 1949 to 1965, and these citations generally do not have accompanying abstracts. The content in PubMed is updated daily.

The links under PubMed Tools and More Resources include MeSH Database, Journals, Database, Single Citation Matcher, and Link Out. The MeSH database is one of the most beneficial features of the PubMed services. When you enter a search term in the query box, the MeSH database displays a list of suggested MeSH terms and entry terms; definitions for the terms are also included. You can build an entire search strategy in the MeSH database and then send the search to PubMed. (For more information on MeSH and the MeSH database, see Chapter 2, as well as the tutorials available online at www.nlm.nih.gov/bsd/disted/pubmed.html.)

One of the most beneficial aspects of PubMed is the ability to look up journals in the journals database. You can search for journals by title, abbreviation, ISSN, and topic, and can also browse the journals by subject terms. NLM assigns subject terms to the journals indexed in MEDLINE to describe the journals' scope. When you search for a journal in the database, it displays the full title, the ISSNs for both the print and electronic versions, the title abbreviation, the year the publication began, the publisher, language, subject terms, and any continuation notes. This information is especially helpful when a patron comes in with an obscure journal abbreviation or wants to know whether a journal is published in English.

The single citation matcher is also helpful when users ask you to help them locate a specific, known article. Using the fill-in-the-blank format, you can enter as much of the citation information as you have available. You can use this feature to find a specific citation, all the works by a certain author, or all items from a particular volume or issue of a journal. When searching for author, you can limit the search to only first author or only last author. The single citation matcher also has an auto-complete feature for journal

PubMed search results

titles and author names. As you enter information, the auto-complete feature will suggest titles or author names.

LinkOut enables libraries to provide links within PubMed to other databases and resources so that users can access the full text when available. More information on LinkOut is available at www.ncbi.nlm.nih.gov/projects/linkout/doc/linkout.html. Also available in PubMed is MyNCBI. MyNCBI is a tool that allows users to register for a free account where they can save PubMed searches, collections of citations, and more. After saving a search to your

MyNCBI account, you can set up automatic email updates when new articles are published that match your search criteria.

For more information on PubMed and PubMed services, take a look at the tutorials available at www.nlm.nih.gov/bsd/disted/pubmed.html.

Cumulative Index to Nursing and Allied Health Literature

Mentioned briefly in Chapter 2, the Cumulative Index to Nursing and Allied Health Literature (CINAHL) is a database originally owned by CINAHL Information Systems but acquired by EBSCO Publishing in 2003. In addition to information on a variety of nursing disciplines, CINAHL includes information on topics such as dentistry, audiology, respiratory therapy, and health information management. More than 3,800 journals are indexed in CINAHL, dating back to 1937. In addition to article citations, the CINAHL database contains Quick Lessons and Evidence-Based Care Sheets. Quick Lessons are two-page summaries of diseases and conditions, each containing a list of references for further information. In addition, all Quick Lessons feature the following sections:

- Description/Etiology
- Facts and Figures
- Risk Factors
- Signs and Symptoms/Clinical Presentation
- Assessment
- Treatment Goals
- Food for Thought
- Red Flags
- What Do I Need to Tell the Patient/Patient's Family?

Written by healthcare professionals at CINAHL Information Systems, Quick Lessons are designed to map to the nursing workflow.

Similar to Quick Lessons, Evidence-Based Care Sheets are one- to two-page overviews of treatment plans for various diseases and conditions. Each Evidence-Based Care Sheet includes sections on "What We Know" and "What We Can Do," with a list of references at the end of each. In addition, there is a coding matrix to rate the references. Categories include published guidelines; general or background information/texts/reports; and policies, procedures, protocols. Evidence-Based Care Sheets are produced and reviewed for accuracy by health professionals at CINAHL Information Systems.

CINAHL also incorporates online continuing education modules that are available within the database. These continuing education units are accredited by the International Association for Continuing Education and Training and are accepted by the American Nurses Association. More information on the CINAHL database, including tutorials and user guides, can be found at support.ebsco.com/cinahl.

Point of Need Resources

MD Consult

Offered by Elsevier, MD Consult (www.mdconsult.com) is a meta-site of medical resources. Within its collection are medical reference books, Clinics of North America (clinical reviews comprising nearly 60 different titles on surgery, medicine, veterinary medicine, nursing, and dentistry), and a slate of full-text journals. It also includes bibliographic databases to other journals, including abstracts from MEDLINE, peer-reviewed practice guidelines, images, news and updates, continuing medical education (CME) offerings, drug information, and customizable patient handouts.

According to its website, almost 2,000 healthcare organizations and 95 percent of U.S. medical schools subscribe to MD Consult. This powerful and easy-to-use tool is very popular with clinicians. It is also very expensive, but both tiered and individual subscriptions are offered. In addition to MD Consult, Elsevier provides numerous products geared toward health sciences professionals, including Nursing Consult, Expert Consult, Procedures Consult, and others.[1]

Why would I want to be a librarian? I haven't been library literate for most of my life. I've always loved books (as objects and for what's in them), but I wasn't very skilled at using libraries for research. I was working on my bachelor of fine arts in painting. When finished, I thought that I would begin working toward a master of fine arts and then find a teaching position. Several major life events slowed that plan to a complete halt!

I instead found myself working in the library of a private Jesuit college. After working with government documents and serials, I ended up as the administrative assistant to the new director of the library. He was a young, dynamic librarian, recruited from out of state. His wife, also a librarian, formerly in the academic arena, began work as a hospital librarian. Spending time around them allowed me a firsthand look at librarianship and leadership in action. In addition, they were in the midst of completing a book on library reference sources to send off to their publisher. Seeing it come out in print was a magical event. Even though I had participated in professional art competitions, won awards, and sold art pieces, I didn't know anyone personally who researched, compiled, and had books published. A year or two passed, and they published two or three more books. Then they told me about a fellowship in medical librarianship being offered at the state university and encouraged me to apply. I was very reluctant at first, but their enthusiasm and confidence in my ability won me over.

I applied for and received the fellowship, and a short time later my 10-year-old son and I drove off north in our little battered VW beetle for unknown adventures! The 12 months of graduate school flew by. For anyone with doubts about starting graduate work in library science, because of being over 30, parenthood status, or temperament (I leaned toward the shier side), do not be discouraged. I met people with all kinds of educational backgrounds from all over the U.S. and the world. I got hands-on use of the latest library information technology of the mid-1980s: database literature searching, which I was immediately drawn to because of its detective-like and problem-solving qualities. It also dawned on me that entering the world of librarianship ensured my place in the new information technology age, as described in the book that I was reading as a class assignment, *Megatrends*. At the time, it reminded me of another book I read while an art student, *The Medium Is the Message*.

I began my medical librarian career at a small clinical branch campus, reporting to the director of the academic library. My library was located off campus in the downtown medical district. It was an excellent first job for a new medical librarian. In the early years, I set up the DOCLINE interlibrary loan system and the Grateful Med end-user searching system to MEDLINE and began offering instructional sessions to the medical students while on the family medicine clerkship. Life was going along well, when suddenly the academic university found that it couldn't support the medical component any longer, so our campus almost closed down. Faculty, staff, and students carried pickets for a while to protest the possible closing. The school of medicine, where the medical students had completed their first two years, then stepped in and agreed to administer our clinical campus. I was asked at that time if I wanted to move to the academic university library or continue with the medical library. I chose the latter—an excellent decision, as it turned out.

Being connected with a large medical library (at the school of medicine) offered tremendous advantages to our campus and medical library. The closer working relationships and knowledge sharing with other medical librarians alone were priceless. With print materials quickly transforming to electronic format, affiliated students, residents, faculty, and staff, through remote access authentication, had access to hundreds of full-text journals and books, and had the ability to search many high-quality databases. So, with added resiliency and energy, I began to focus on coordinating instructional sessions for the family medicine residents, especially the new interns. They came to our program from all over the world and possessed varying degrees of medical literature searching experience. Refresher or beginning classes in using PubMed and navigating the remote access system were offered at orientation, at noon conferences, and other times during their three-year residency program. Spur of the moment teaching sessions were encouraged. How to put together a search strategy to retrieve the best, most reliable information for patient care, education, or research needs was one of the most important goals.

Working in a smaller health sciences library has allowed me more freedom, at times, to explore and implement some nontraditional library services, such as the purchase of multiple copies of medical exam and review books for use by students and residents. It started out as an experiment, more or less accidentally, and now has the blessing of the assistant dean. Being in a smaller setting has allowed me the opportunity to establish closer working relationships with the clinical clerkship directors and other clinical faculty members by serving on committees with them, meeting with them formally and informally, communicating regularly through email and newsletters, and always having an open door for their unexpected visits and requests. The assistant dean regularly comes to the library to meet with students and residents and to talk with me and my staff. He often leaves me with an interesting research or patient care request to work on.

I have my former boss, the library director, and his wife to thank for opening up the world of librarianship to me. Now seems to be one of the most exciting times to be entering the librarian profession. There is a sense of openness and a desire for creativity that I don't remember existing 20 years ago. At one time, if you chose to work in a smaller or more remote library setting, it was a cause for concern because of distance from colleagues and difficulty attending national meetings. Now, it can be a cause for celebration! Being connected to your colleagues, continuing education, and all the other educational and fun aspects of librarianship may only be a podcast, blog, wiki, or the next new informational technology away.

Lee Clemans-Taylor is Director and Librarian at the J. Ellis Sparks, M.D. Medical Library at the Huntsville Regional Medical Campus (main.uab.edu/uasom/2/show.asp?durki=20025).

UpToDate

UpToDate (www.uptodate.com) is an evidence-based and peer reviewed resource that markets itself as a unique resource for clinicians, patients, and a worldwide clinical community. According to the website, "Every day, clinicians have questions about patient care. Patients have questions about their health as well. Why not recruit a faculty of experts to answer those questions, keep the information updated, and create a format that is easy to use? Why not also provide all of the necessary background information to understand why the recommendations are being made?"[2] The content in UpToDate is written by clinicians who serve as authors, editors, and reviewers for the resource by monitoring and synthesizing the content of more than 400 journals. UpToDate includes more than 7,000 topics in 13 specialties and is intended to provide practicing clinicians information at the point of care. Accidental hospital librarians are the most likely to encounter UpToDate.

PDA Resources

The health sciences are driven by technology, and one of the main problem areas for information and health sciences professionals is how to take advantage of all the electronic resources available to clinicians at the point of care. In other words, how do you put the power of PubMed or the almost 3,000-page *Harrison's Principles of Internal Medicine* in the palm of the clinicians' hands at their patients' bedsides? One answer is by using PDAs. PDAs and other handheld computer devices are becoming more and more commonplace in the healthcare setting. Healthcare professionals can use their PDAs to synchronize wirelessly with the hospital network, allowing them to get immediate updates on their patients. These devices are in fact so useful and so popular that some health sciences programs require students to buy them before they can even start classes. Health sciences librarians need to learn about PDAs and the different information and research resources available for them. For one example, see the 2006 article "Circulating PDAs: A Hospital Libraries Experience," in which Cathy Eames describes how her library helped her hospital's department of pediatrics provide PDAs (and support for those PDAs) to 105 pediatric residents.[3]

Users can access information through their PDAs in two ways: They can connect to the internet through a wireless connection, or they can download applications to the PDA in order to access information without worrying about connections or firewalls. How the information or application actually gets downloaded to the PDA in the first place, however, depends on what is being downloaded and on the model of PDA that is being used. While Palm OS and Pocket PC are currently the most common operating systems for PDAs, many resources are also becoming available for BlackBerry devices and iPhones. The price of these resources also varies by vendor, but you can find a number of really useful free resources. Here are just a few examples of some of the different kinds of resources that are available for PDAs—just remember this is in no way a complete list!

NLM Mobile

The NLM has a number of different projects geared toward mobile devices (www.nlm.nih.gov/mobile) and provides these to the healthcare community for free:

- PubMed for Handhelds (pubmedhh.nlm.nih.gov/nlm) is simply a website designed for optimal viewing on PDA screens. This means that most of the bells and whistles on the regular PubMed site have been stripped away so that the meat of the site can display quickly and easily.

- AIDSinfo's PDA Tools (aidsinfo.nih.gov/PDATools/Default. aspx?MenuItem=AIDSinfoTools) provides for download of the federally approved HIV treatment and prevention guidelines as well as the current treatment regimens for HIV infection and AIDS-related illnesses, including the prevention of HIV transmission from occupational exposure and mother-to-child transmission during pregnancy. The information is free; users just need to have Adobe Reader installed on their PDA.

- Handheld Computer Resources in the NCBI Bookshelf (www.ncbi.nlm.nih.gov/entrez/query/Books.live/Help/ mobile.html) provides some NCBI books for download. To view these, users first need to download a free version of Mobipocket Reader (www.mobipocket.com/en/ DownloadSoft/DownLoadReaderStep1.asp).

- Radiation Event Medical Management (REMM): Guidance on Diagnosis & Treatment for Health Care Providers (remm.nlm.gov/Aboutthissite.htm) is a free resource intended to provide "just-in-time, evidence based, usable information with sufficient background and context to make complex issues understandable to those *without* formal radiation medicine expertise."[4]

- Wireless Information System for Emergency Responders (WISER; wiser.nlm.nih.gov) is designed to assist first responders in hazardous material incidents.[5]

Epocrates Rx

Epocrates Rx (www.epocrates.com) is a popular drug resource with a good deal of free content, including drug-related monographs and formularies. A one-year subscription to the more comprehensive Epocrates Essential includes information on 3,300 different

National Library of Medicine mobile options

drugs, 1,200 different diseases, medical formulas, hundreds of diagnostic tests, and other tools. Find a comparison of the different subscription levels at www.epocrates.com/products/comparison_ table.html. Individuals can purchase the resource, or organizations can purchase multiple licenses.

Diagnosaurus

Diagnosaurus (books.mcgraw-hill.com/medical/diagnosaurus) is a differential diagnosis tool provided free by McGraw-Hill. Download the software, then search by disease, symptom, or organ system.

Essential Evidence Plus

Essential Evidence Plus (www.essentialevidenceplus.com) is an evidenced-based point-of-care resource for clinicians. Included in the resource are Patient-Oriented Evidence that Matters (POEMS), Cochrane abstracts, evidence-based medicine (EBM) guidelines, a variety of calculators, Derm expert, and more.

Skyscape

In addition to these individual examples, some companies provide multiple health sciences related PDA resources. One such vendor is Skyscape, Inc. (www.skyscape.com), which specializes in mobile medical technology. Some of its resources are completely free, and a list can be found on the Skyscape website at www.sky scape.com/estore/store.aspx?Category=35.

The sheer number of PDA tools for healthcare professionals is overwhelming. Health sciences librarians needn't learn how to work all these different tools. By doing what librarians do best, though— finding, evaluating, and providing access to PDA resources—health sciences librarians have a real opportunity to demonstrate their tech savvy and how in touch they are with what is going on in the clinical world. You might start by creating a website listing relevant PDA resources, such as the one at the Florida State University College of Medicine (med.fsu.edu/library/PDASoftware.asp). Also, be sure to ask about PDA access and applications when negotiating licenses for other electronic resources. Regularly peruse the "PDAs @ the Library" column in the *Journal of Electronic Resources in Medical Libraries* to get ideas on how to use PDA resources.

Evidence-Based Medicine Resources

Cochrane Library

Part of the Cochrane Collaboration (www.cochrane.org), the Cochrane Library (www.thecochranelibrary.com) is a collection of EBM resources. Published by Wiley-Blackwell, it is updated on a quarterly basis and available on CD-ROM as well as on the web.

	FLORIDA STATE UNIVERSITY	COLLEGE OF MEDICINE

Charlotte Edwards Maguire Medical Library

Off-Campus Access (EZProxy) | For New Users | Inter-Library Loan | Medical Matrix | Google | Ask a Librarian

Medical Library Home >> PDA Websites - PDA Software

PDA Websites

TOPICS

PDA Hardware
Instructional Sites
PDA SOFTWARE
Software Archive Sites
Software Developers

CoM PDA Instructions

PDA SOFTWARE

CATEGORY		PALM	POCKET PC	$
Backup Software	Backup Buddy	x		
Billing	PocketBilling	x	x	
	Remedy	x		
Cholesterol Management Tools	ATPIII	x		Free
	Essential Evidence Plus (InfoRetriever) *(Student Handout)* *(Faculty Handout)* *(Handout for Palms)*	x	x	
	Stat Cholesterol	x		Free
Clinical Prediction Tools	Essential Evidence Plus (InfoRetriever) *(Student Handout)* *(Faculty Handout)* *(Handout for Palms)*	x	x	Trial
	MedRules	x		Free

Florida State University College of Medicine PDA websites list

The Cochrane Library comprises six databases: Cochrane Database of Systematic Reviews (CDSR); Database of Abstracts of Reviews of Effects (DARE); Cochrane Central Register of Controlled Trials (CENTRAL); Cochrane Methodology Register (CMR); Health Technology Assessment Database (HTA); and NHS Economic Evaluation Database (NHSEED).

The CDSR contains almost 4,000 reviews and almost 2,000 protocols. These systematic reviews list all known references to trials for specific interventions. This database also includes the Cochrane Database of Methodology Reviews, which are systematic reviews of methodological studies, as well as systematic reviews of studies on the accuracy of diagnostic tests. Abstracts and summaries of reviews can be browsed for free on the Cochrane Library website.

DARE, created by the University of York's Centre for Reviews and Dissemination, is made up of more than 3,000 systematic reviews, which are assessed for their quality. According to the publisher, DARE "is a key resource for busy decision makers and can be used for answering questions about the effects of specific interventions, whether such questions arise from practice or when making policy."[6]

CENTRAL is a database of information about published articles on controlled, clinical trials. While it does not contain the full text of these articles, CENTRAL does list the title, publication information, and a summary. Much of the information in CENTRAL is gathered from MEDLINE and EMBASE, a bibliographic database particularly robust in drug and pharmaceutical research articles. Many of the records in CENTRAL link to the corresponding record in PubMed.

Similar to CENTRAL, CMR lists publications that report on the methods used in controlled trials. All CMR records contain bibliographic details for each article.

Also produced by the Centre for Reviews and Dissemination, HTA consists of studies on the assessment of health technology, including "medical, social, ethical and economic implications of healthcare interventions."[7] The purpose of HTA is to improve the cost-effectiveness of healthcare around the world.

NHSEED is similar to HTA in that the goal is to improve cost-effectiveness. With more than 5,000 abstracts, NHSEED "assists decision-makers by systematically identifying economic evaluations from around the world, appraising their quality and highlighting their relative strengths and weaknesses."[8]

The Cochrane Library provides a wealth of information for EBM. Searches can be conducted in just one database or across all of them, and there are links to MEDLINE abstracts. A number of tutorials and user guides, in English as well as various other languages, are located on the web at www3.interscience.wiley.com/cgi-bin/mrwhome/106568753/HELP_Cochrane.html.[9]

National Guideline Clearinghouse

The National Guideline Clearinghouse (NGC; www.guidelines.gov) is a free database of evidence-based clinical practice guidelines.[10] Produced by the Agency for Healthcare Research and Quality of the U.S. Department of Health and Human Services, NGC was originally created in conjunction with the American Medical Association and the American Association of Health Plans. NGC's purpose is to provide healthcare providers with "objective, detailed information on clinical practice guidelines and to further their dissemination, implementation and use."[11] Each guideline features a structured abstract, links to the full text, PDA downloads, comparisons with other guidelines, a bibliography, guideline syntheses, and an expert commentary. Guidelines are available for a variety of diseases, conditions, treatments, and interventions. Guidelines can be browsed by disease name and treatment measures, as well as by the producing organization and overall index. NGC uses MeSH (discussed in Chapter 2) to index diseases and conditions.

TRIP Database

Established in 1997, the Turning Research into Practice Database (TRIP; www.tripdatabase.com) is a free resource based in the U.K. and designed to assist clinicians in locating EBM materials on the internet. This database "has evolved into a sophisticated tool for locating the highest possible evidence with which to inform clinical decisions, using the principles of evidence based medicine."[12] In addition to other sources, TRIP searches MEDLINE through PubMed. TRIP also provides medical images and patient education handouts, as well as a section of EBM links. These links are divided into three categories: EBM Resources, What Is Evidence-Based Medicine?, and Practicing EBM. From there, the categories are divided into subcategories. Resources available here include EBM calculators, organizations, an introduction to EBM, and tips on topics such as how to conduct a search for EBM, how to formulate clinical questions, and how to read a scientific paper. Information on the TRIP Database is available at its website as well as the TRIP blog called Liberating the Literature (blog.tripdata base.com).[13]

Specialized Databases and Resources

NORD Rare Disease Database

The National Organization for Rare Disorders (NORD; www.rare diseases.org) is a group of health organizations and associations that strives to help people with rare, or "orphan," diseases. NORD provides a number of services, including the Rare Disease Database, a database of reports covering 1,150 diseases. The reports are written by either NORD physicians or NORD medical writers. If written by a medical writer, the reports are reviewed by physicians. Each report contains a listing of organizations related to the particular disease, making this an excellent resource for consumer health questions. The search functionality, however, isn't very fancy; for instance, neither "Meniere's" or "Menieres" maps to "Meniere." However, an alphabetical listing of all the diseases is provided, so if you feel that what you are looking for should be included, be sure to browse the listing. Subscriptions are offered, but anyone can search the database and purchase single reports for less than $10.

OncologySTAT

Provided by Elsevier, OncologySTAT (www.oncologystat.com) is a free web-based resource for cancer information and research. OncologySTAT features full-text access to more than 100 cancer-related journals from Elsevier, as well as journal scans and customizable CME programs. Other content includes "What Your Patients Are Reading," summaries of cancer-related news in the media and on the internet; an integrated MEDLINE search; and downloadable patient education handouts. Content is organized by cancer type and by category. Anyone can access OncologySTAT, and additional features are available after registering.

Health Sciences Online

Launched in September 2008, Health Sciences Online (www.hso. info) brings together more than 50,000 resources on a variety of health sciences topics. Founding partners include the Centers for Disease Control and Prevention (CDC), World Bank, American College of Preventive Medicine, University of British Columbia, and World Health Organization (WHO), among others. According to the Health Sciences Online website, "Health sciences information and training are vital for health and socioeconomic development, but excellent, free learning resources are difficult to find. In recent years, information and communication technologies, particularly the internet, have been central to remedying this situation. But there are still significant hurdles to accessing online content. WHO and others have shown that there is an enormous need to identify selective, current, accessible online educational and training resources to promote appropriate care and policies."[14] Divided into categories such as guidelines/handbooks, ebooks, courses, lectures/presentations, reports, and videos, all of the freely available resources included on Health Sciences Online are carefully selected by clinicians and healthcare providers.

SportDiscus

Published by the Sport Information Resource Center, SportDiscus (www.sirc.ca/products/sportdiscus.cfm) is a bibliographic database for fitness, sports, and sports medicine topics, as well as workplace wellness, coaching and training, and physical education. It contains the full text of more than 400 journals in addition to book chapters, theses and dissertations, conference proceedings, and websites. While many health sciences librarians may never use SportDiscus, this resource can be especially beneficial for librarians working as liaisons to athletic training or sports medicine departments or for those in academic libraries.

ERIC

Education Resources Information Center (ERIC; www.eric.ed.gov) is a great database to search when you are looking for information related to education. Sponsored by the U.S. Department of Education's Institute of Education Sciences, it includes articles, books, conference papers, technical reports, and more. ERIC is especially helpful in locating gray literature such as conference proceedings, research reports, and the like.

EMBASE

Produced by Elsevier, EMBASE (short for Excerpta Medica Database) is a bibliographic database of more than 19 million biomedical and pharmacological citations and abstracts. It is international in scope and can be especially helpful when you are looking for information on new drugs or pharmaceuticals research. Citations are indexed using EMTREE and Elsevier's Life Science thesaurus, and also include MeSH terms as synonyms. In addition to unique EMBASE records, the database also incorporates MEDLINE records. For more information about EMBASE, see the User Support section of EMBASE.com (info.embase.com/user_support/learning_tools.shtml).

The Art of Negotiation

If you are responsible for licensing content, get ready for sticker shock. Health sciences resources are really expensive. Make sure you communicate with stakeholders so that you know the types of resources they need. The best, shiniest, newest database may be great—but if it isn't what your people need, then you've wasted money. Make sure your stakeholders understand that if you buy really expensive database X, then you won't be able to get database Y. And once you purchase it, market it! Make sure people know you have access, and offer training.

Before you buy anything, first check with your IT people to make sure people can actually get to the resource, especially if you work in a hospital or clinic. The best electronic resource is worthless if it is blocked by IT.

Lastly, never be afraid to negotiate; you don't have to accept the first price a vendor offers. Tell the salesperson that it's too much, and you can't pay that. You don't have anything to lose by trying to get a better deal. Licensing is scary, but luckily there are all sorts of good resources to help you. You may want to check out Liblicense (www.library.yale.edu/~llicense) to help you get started as well as the Recommended Reading section at the end of this book.

Endnotes

1. For a complete listing of health sciences products, visit the Elsevier site (www.elsevier.com/wps/find/subject_area_browse.cws_home?sh1State =-0&sh2State=&SH0Only=HS).

2. UpToDate, "About UpToDate," www.utdol.com/home/about/index. html

3. Cathy Eames, "Circulating PDAs: A Hospital Libraries Experience," *Journal of Hospital Librarianship* 6 (2006): 95–101.

4. Radiation Event Medical Management, "About This Site," remm.nlm. gov/Aboutthissite.htm

5. For more information, see a review of the database: Kathryn Skhal, "Wireless Information System for Emergency Responders (WISER)," *Journal of the Medical Library Association* 94, no. 1 (Jan. 2006): 97.

6. The Cochrane Library, "Product Descriptions," www3.interscience. wiley.com/cgi-bin/mrwhome/106568753/ProductDescriptions.html? CRETRY=1&SRETRY=0

7. Ibid.

8. Ibid.

9. For more information, see a review of the database: Roberta Bronson Fitzpatrick, "The Cochrane Library via Wiley InterScience," *Journal of Electronic Resources in Medical Libraries* 2, no. 4 (Dec. 2005): 99–113.

10. National Guideline Clearinghouse, "NGC Mission Statement," www.guidelines.gov/about/mission.aspx

11. Also see a review of the database: Roberta Bronson Fitzpatrick, "The National Guideline Clearinghouse," *Journal of Electronic Resources in Medical Libraries* 4, no. 3 (2007): 99–112.

12. TRIP Database, "Introduction to the TRIP Process," www.tripdata base.com/aboutus/tripprocess.html

13. For more information, see a review of the database: Trina Fyfe, "Turning Research Into Practice (TRIP) Database," *Journal of the Medical Library Association* 95, no. 2 (April 2007): 215–216.

14. Health Sciences Online, "About HSO," hso.info/about/about.html

Chapter 6

Resources and Networking

Join the local MLA chapter, attend the meetings, talk with working librarians. Volunteer. "Just do it.
—Survey Respondent

If you've found yourself working as an accidental health sciences librarian, you'll want to seek out colleagues, resources, continuing education opportunities, and professional development possibilities that will help you learn your new field, make new friends, network, and check out the field. You've gotten the job—now, you need to be able to do the job and to make informed career decisions. One of the best aspects of health librarianship is that it is a big enough field to have a plethora of opportunities, as well as some very narrow specialized opportunities. This chapter will point you to where health sciences librarians "live," both physically and virtually.

Associations

Let's start by talking about finding an association to call home. Library associations are great places to meet people, learn new things, network, and get involved in the profession—but you have to be *actively* involved, either physically or virtually. Just paying your dues and saying "I'm a member" doesn't do you much good. While you might "lurk" for a bit when trying to choose the right association (or associations) for you and your career goals, once you choose, you need to get involved. Most association memberships aren't cheap, so take full advantage of what they offer and get the most for your money. Try to think of this as an investment in your *career*, not just your *job*. As one survey respondent explains, "The medical library associations are much more useful to me because of the benefits of professional networking and the cumulative knowledgebase of the membership."

If your institution provides no support for travel or continuing education, then factor this into your decision about which association(s) to join. Many state and regional organizations are excellent associations, and many provide very good and reasonably priced programs. If your institution isn't able to provide funding for travel, try to at least negotiate for administrative leave to attend conferences and programs. Also, be sure to tie what you do at your job to the things you learned at each conference or continuing education event. When you are able to draw a clear picture of the benefits to the organization from what you learned at a conference, you may be able to convince your employer to find some travel money next time. If nothing else, by making this investment in your career, you may very well meet your next boss—one who may have plenty of travel money. Even if you can't find a way to attend annual meetings or conferences, though, you can still be involved. Association work goes on in the virtual world year round, and volunteers are always needed.

Medical Library Association

Founded in 1898, the Medical Library Association (MLA; www.mlanet.org) is the mother-ship association for health sciences librarianship. Don't let the name fool you, though—all flavors of health sciences people, more than 4,000 of them, are welcomed here.[1] The Accidental Health Sciences Librarian Survey asked to what professional organizations respondents belonged. Of the 319 respondents from the U.S., 274 (86 percent) reported they were MLA members. Of the 45 (14 percent) who reported they weren't members of MLA, 25 (56 percent) of them were members of one of the regional chapters of MLA—leaving 6.3 percent, or just 20, of the 319 respondents as having no involvement in MLA at all. Survey respondents noted that "MLA and its members have been great mentors in my library career" and that MLA is "focused on supporting the health services librarian" and is "great for keeping [members] informed on medical library issues." MLA offers continuing education opportunities throughout the year, such as webcasts, teleconferences, and an independent reading program, as well as courses at the annual meeting. It also offers a professional journal—the *Journal of the Medical Library Association*—and professional resources including information on library benchmarking, advocacy, standards, and accreditation.

MLA has 14 chapters, or regional associations. Chapters are good ways to get involved without having to join the national MLA; you don't have to be a member of MLA to join an MLA chapter. Survey respondents overwhelmingly said that their chapters were their favorite association. One person likes her local chapter best because it is smaller and she can "network with other librarians better without feeling overwhelmed." Someone else mentioned that her regional chapter is her favorite association because it contains "job-pertinent information, but [is] regional, so I can get to know the other librarians," while another wrote that chapters are "essential for keeping up with medical librarianship and for networking." MLA chapters are listed in Appendix C.

In addition to chapters, MLA offers membership in sections and special interest groups (SIGs), which are more ad hoc and subject to fewer governance requirements than sections are. A full list of each can be found in Appendix C. Sections include Consumer and Patient Health Information, Hospital Libraries, Cancer Librarians, and more. Like sections, SIGs "provide a forum for members with unique interests to identify and meet with others with similar interests."[2] SIGs include Vision Science, Pediatric Libraries,

Libraries in Curriculum, and Department of Veterans Affairs Librarians, among others.

State Associations

As with the smaller regional MLA chapters, state health sciences library associations are great places to get involved. As one survey respondent acknowledged, "My favorite is the state group because I can foster change locally much more easily than nationally." Another mentioned that "my favorite association is the state health sciences librarians association because of the close knit feeling of the association, the ability for librarians working in different regions of the state to work together and learn from each other, the many opportunities for networking that just seem to work better than bigger organizations." A list of state health sciences library associations appears in Appendix C.

Other Associations

A number of other associations may be beneficial for accidental health sciences librarians. As you can see, there is a professional association, section, or SIG for virtually any topic or interest. Some of these are:

- American Association of Colleges of Pharmacy—
  Libraries/Educational Resources Section,
  www.aacp.org/governance/SECTIONS/library
  educationalresources/Pages/default.aspx

- American Medical Informatics Association (AMIA),
  www.amia.org

- American Society for Information Science & Technology
  (ASIST)—Medical Informatics SIG,
  www.asis.org/SIG/med.html

- Association of Academic Health Sciences Libraries,
  www.aahsl.org

- Association of Mental Health Librarians, www.mhlib.org

- Canadian Health Libraries Association, www.chla-absc.ca

- Health and Science Communications Association, www.hesca.org

- International Federation of Library Associations and Institutions—Health and Biosciences Libraries Section, www.ifla.org/VII/s28

- Libraries in Medical Education SIG of the Association of American Medical Colleges' Groups on Educational Affairs, www.aahsl.org/mc/page.do?sitePageId=84885

- National Network of Libraries of Medicine (NN/LM), nnlm.gov

- Public Library Association (PLA), www.ala.org/ala/mgrps/divs/pla

- Special Libraries Association (SLA)—Biomedical and Life Sciences Division, units.sla.org/division/dbio

- SLA—Biomedical and Life Sciences Division, Medical Section, units.sla.org/division/dbio/medicalsection

How did I develop into the Librarian/Information Guru/Go-To person that I am today? The same as many of you: lots of subject interests, but one strong drive to capture information and find creative ways to share it. Doesn't quite fit the stereotypical "keeper of the books" image, right? I'm the type of person who says, "Here, let me show you how to find this or use that resource." I love those "Aha!" moments, when you can see that the customer "gets it"—and that you've created another loyal library supporter.

How was I fortunate enough to become a health sciences librarian? Mostly by being in the right place at the right time when a hospital decided to hire its first-ever full-time librarian. The rewards of working in a health-related setting cover a wide range, from getting critical treatment details into the hands of an emergency room physician to training resident physicians and students in other health-profession fields how to critically assess information in the medical literature to providing key information for a new drug being reviewed by the FDA.

The drive to organize information and materials hit me early. By third grade (8 years old) I was a library aide—did the shelving, showed people how to use the card catalog, etc. By the time I got to college, I had 10 years' experience as a library and media aide in school! A fascination with the history and evolution of languages led to a BA in linguistics, then on to library school and my MLIS (back when the computer course meant typing stacks of batch cards and hard wiring a motherboard with a soldering iron). I was determined *not* to be the type of "professional librarian" I had experienced in public and university settings—the ones with the "you are disturbing me" look and who told people to "find it yourself." Luckily, I'd had some very nurturing role models, especially that elementary school librarian who told me I was "a born librarian."

I've been a public, hospital, academic medical center/ faculty, and now pharmaceutical R&D [research and development] librarian for more than 30 years. I have found that, despite the learning curve at each new job, the same set of skills and personality traits are pertinent. A strong sense of curiosity and enthusiasm about sharing what I've learned has always been an asset. (It's also fun to shatter the stereotype. I was shushed for whistling and singing—quietly, of course—in the medical school library where I worked, sang in an on-campus rock band, and had my own AM radio show in my undergraduate days.) The ability to keep the flow of information going both ways still works in the current setting of some training happening via webcasts—can't see my audience but try to keep them entertained while they learn, using an upbeat attitude and high level of enthusiasm. The feedback emails frequently include comments such as "can tell you're passionate about what you do."

That really sums it up in a word: *passion*. If you love what you do, the enthusiasm is contagious, and your customers are more likely to return. How can you keep the high energy level? By making obstacles become challenges and finding new ways to grab the attention and support of your clientele.

Challenges run the gamut, from budget and space cutbacks to closure of some hospital and pharmaceutical company libraries. It's not all "free on the internet." How can you fight back? Hopefully, you've already laid the groundwork by making your services indispensable to the professionals you support. Moving to another region of the country is not always an option, but reinventing your self-perception and finding new ways to apply your skills in the same or a different institution is possible. Apply that passion and expertise to a new area—marketing, health administration, business opportunity analysis, and competitive intelligence are just examples.

Mindy Robinson-Paquette is Senior Information Specialist at Sanofi-aventis U.S. (www.sanofi-aventis. us) in Malvern, Pennsylvania.

Blogs

One of the best ways to keep up with and find out what's going on in the health sciences library profession is by reading blogs and websites. You can find a health sciences library blog for every interest. The MLA provides a list of its blogs and wikis under Web 2.0 Resources (www.mlanet.org/resources/web20_resources.html); this page also lists the blogs and RSS feeds for MLA sections, chapters, and SIGs, as well as those for other health sciences library associations. There is even a blog for the *Journal of the Medical Library Association*, JMLA Case Studies in Health Sciences Librarianship (jmlacasestudies.blogspot.com). The NN/LM hosts blogs for its regional news (nnlm.gov/news).

In addition to organizations, individual health sciences libraries host a multitude of blogs on various topics, such as these:

- Bioinformatics @ Becker: Updates and Musings from the Bioinformatics Team at Becker Medical Library, beckerinfo.net/bioinformatics

- Botsford Hospital Library Blog, www.botsford.org/ library/blog

- Dental Information & Library Innovation: News and Tips about Dentistry from the University of Michigan Dental

Informationist (and friends), mblog.lib.umich.edu/
dentlib

- Maine Medical Center Library, mmclibrary.wordpress.
  com

- Northern Virginia Community College Medical Education
  Campus Library, medicalcampuslibrary.blogspot.com

- Spokane Public Library Health Blog,
  new.spokanelibrary.org/blog/health

Dental Information & Library Innovation blog

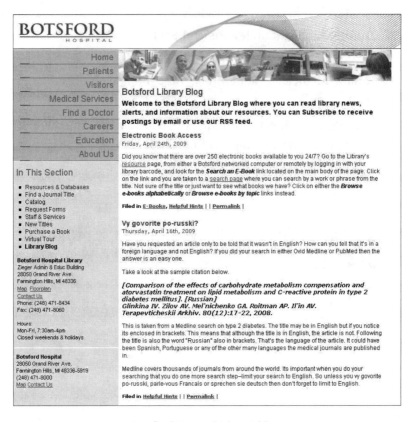

Botsford Hospital Library blog

A number of health sciences librarians have personal blogs as well. Our survey found that an overwhelming percentage of respondents regularly read:

- davidrothman.net: Exploring Medical Librarianship and Web Geekery, davidrothman.net

- Krafty Librarian, www.kraftylibrarian.com

Though certainly not inclusive, a list of blogs related to health sciences librarianship is available at liswiki.org/wiki/Medlib_ Blogs.

Northern Virginia Community College
Medical Education Campus Library blog

RSS Feeds

Non-blog RSS feeds are another good way to keep up with what's happening in the field, and the National Library of Medicine (NLM) maintains several. Take a look at the list of NLM RSS Feeds for News, Podcasts, and Webcasts (www.nlm.nih.gov/listserv/rss_podcasts.html). This site also includes links explaining what RSS feeds are and how to set one up.

MLA provides an RSS feed for MLA News (feeds.feedburner.com/MedicalLibraryAssociationNews), in addition to some of the other feeds available from their list of Web 2.0 Resources. You can also sign up for RSS feeds for individual journals to receive alerts on new articles, tables of contents, and more. The Ebling Library for the Health Sciences at the University of Wisconsin–Madison provides a list (ebling.library.wisc.edu/rss) of electronic journal feeds by topic and by title; the library also maintains a list of health news feeds and podcasts.

You may also want to check out "RSS4Lib: Innovative Ways Libraries Use RSS" (www.rss4lib.com). This blog, started in 2005 by Ken Varnum at the University of Michigan Libraries, features posts about RSS topics that are specific to libraries.

Literature

Books

For those interested in learning more about the history of health sciences librarianship, Jennifer Connor's *Guardians of Medical Knowledge: The Genesis of the Medical Library Association* (Scarecrow, 2000) and Wyndham D. Miles' *History of the National Library of Medicine: The Nation's Treasury of Medical Knowledge* (www.nlm.nih.gov/hmd/manuscripts/miles/miles.html) are excellent places to start. Though published 10 years ago, *The Medical Library Association Guide to Managing Health Care Libraries* (Neal-Schuman, 2000) provides a useful framework for new health sciences librarians and is still relevant today. This work gives an overview of the healthcare environment and healthcare libraries, as well as basics on administration, collection development, and access to resources, in addition to financial management and human resources management.

To find out what is going on in health sciences librarianship today, you can consult a variety of books. For technology, take a look at *Internet Cool Tools for Physicians,* by Melissa L. Rethlefsen, David L. Rothman, and Daniel S. Mojon (Springer, 2009). M. Sandra Wood's *Medical Librarian 2.0: Use of Web 2.0 Technologies in Reference Services* (Haworth, 2007) is also worth a look. Librarians dealing with patient education and consumer health should examine Michele Spatz's *Answering Consumer Health Questions: The Medical Library Association Guide for Reference*

Librarians (Neal-Schuman, 2008) or Marge Kars' and Lynda Baker's *The Medical Library Association Guide to Health Literacy* (Neal-Schuman, 2008). Those involved in or interested in technical services roles may want to browse Linda Walton's *Collection Development and Management for Electronic, Audiovisual, and Print Resources in Health Sciences Libraries* (MLA, 2004). Those new to health sciences librarianship (and library and information science educators) may want to review Woods' *Introduction to Health Sciences Librarianship* (Haworth, 2008). Now in its fifth edition, *Introduction to Reference Sources in the Health Sciences* (Neal-Schuman, 2008) is the standard introductory text for health sciences reference sources. It deals with all aspects of reference sources including collection management, drug information, consumer health sources, statistics, directories, and grant sources.

Journals

You can find a journal to fill any niche of health sciences librarianship. The open-access *Journal of the Medical Library Association* publishes articles on a variety of health sciences librarianship issues. Regular contents include original research papers, case studies, brief communications, electronic resource reviews, and book reviews. *Medical Reference Services Quarterly* has original research articles as well as sections on Navigat[ing] the Net, Online Updates: A Column for Search Analysts, Hospital Information Services, and Informatics Education. The *Journal of Electronic Resources in Medical Libraries* examines all aspects of electronic resources, including topics such as discussions with vendors, ejournals, "ecore" lists, and PDAs @ the Library. The *Journal of Consumer Health on the Internet*, a publication for "librarians and health information providers [to] describe programs and services aimed at helping patients and the general public find the health information they need,"[3] is also a good choice. Columns include Health Sitings, Alternative & Complementary Therapies, Editor's

Select Sites, Health Literacy, and WebHealth Topics. The *Journal of Hospital Librarianship*, aimed at primarily hospital and clinical librarians, discusses consumer health and patient education issues, international libraries, research, technology, and the web. For international perspectives on health sciences librarianship, check out *Health Information and Libraries Journal*. Journals that may also be of interest include the *Journal of the Canadian Health Libraries Association*, *Journal of the American Medical Informatics Association*, and *Biomedical Digital Libraries*.

It is also helpful to read general library journals that are not necessarily geared toward the health sciences. *Library Journal*, *Computers in Libraries*, *Journal of the American Society for Information Science and Technology*, *Library Hi Tech*, *Online*, and *Searcher* appeared most often on the survey responses.

Many respondents to the survey felt that it would be more beneficial for health sciences librarians to read the medical literature than the library literature. One person said, "I'm reading mostly what is going on in the field I work with and support. [I read] some library, but not much—library literature is speaking to what used to be and was, not what is coming and is." The *Journal of Medical Internet Research*, *Journal of the American Medical Association*, *New England Journal of Medicine*, and *Medicine on the Net* were the publications most frequently mentioned throughout the survey responses.

Newsletters

A number of newsletters will help you keep up with the world of health sciences librarianship. *MLA News* provides updates on association activities and happenings in the profession, such as continuing education events, employment opportunities, technology, and internet resources. Many chapters and sections have newsletters as well, so you can keep up with goings on. You can find searching information and updates on NLM databases in the *NLM Technical Bulletin*.

When I finished school, I did not know "what I wanted to do when I grew up." I took college classes part-time. Job interest tests were inconclusive. I married and had children; college was ignored for 10 years. I worked in a hospital for 20 years and finished my undergraduate degree in business at the same time the hospital laid me off due to cutbacks. I learned I am a generalist—good at many things, but not specializing in any one.

I found a position assisting physicians with research. Finally, I realized that my talents were ideal for a librarian. Being a librarian is perfect for the generalist. I enjoy working in the health sciences, and when I took my MLIS, I focused on special librarian classes.

As a new health sciences librarian, I've learned that keeping up in the field is one of my greatest challenges. The medical field is constantly redefining itself and its practices. The research staff in my company create medical guidelines based on the best evidence-based medical information available. Every year they examine the current literature to see what's new and what is best practice. This research is then used by practitioners in offices and hospitals as they care for their patients.

I have to be aware of the work being done within multiple health fields through the national associations of the different disciplines. I need to know what new information is available from the Centers for Disease Control and Prevention (CDC). When a new medical practice guideline is released from different agencies (private and government), the medical staff wants to see how it applies to its current research. The major journals in each field have to be monitored as new issues are released.

I should stay current in available internet tools. Much of our research can be done through the internet because we have some good resources available in the U.S. like MEDLINE and PubMed. If I can set up an automatic email notification or RSS feed when the American College of Obstetrics and Gynecology releases new information, I'll see that quickly rather than having to maintain a weekly or monthly schedule to check its site to see what is new. I can use social bookmarks such as Delicious to tag different medical search engines quickly, then bring them up together for myself or for a colleague. If training is needed, I can use a program like Google Docs to share the training documents. The important thing is knowing what tools are available and how they may be used.

Finally, I need to keep up with fellow librarians, both medical and nonmedical. There are some excellent blogs maintained by medical librarians (davidrothman.net and the Krafty Librarian are very informative and friendly). The different library associations excel in providing information. The MLA is specific to health sciences librarians and provides an email list for day-to-day information and communication in the field. The MLA offers continuing education, mentors, conferences, books, online articles, and the *Journal of the Medical Library Association*—all resources to help me stay current in the field. Each national association has similar tools available.

Vicki Crom is Librarian at Milliman Care Guidelines LLC (www.careguidelines.com) in San Diego, California.

Lists

MLA hosts several lists that may be of interest. MEDLIB-L is an open email discussion list that anyone can join and focuses on discussion of topics of interest to medical and health sciences librarians. According to MLA, MEDLIB-L "provides a forum for MLA members and other health sciences information professionals to discuss important issues about administrating their libraries and developing their careers."[4] MLA-FOCUS provides current updates and announcements on MLA. Unlike MEDLIB-L, however, MLA-FOCUS is limited to MLA members. There is also an MLA-STUDENT list that is open to all library and information science students. An Expert Searching list, provided by MLA's Public Services Section, discusses health sciences librarians' roles in "the expert retrieval and evaluation of information in support of knowledge and evidence-based clinical, scientific, and administrative decision making at all health institutions, and the role of librarians in training future health sciences practitioners and other end users in the best retrieval methods for knowledge-based practice, research, and lifelong learning."[5] A list of MLA lists is available at www.mlanet.org/discussion. In addition to these, most MLA chapters, SIGs, and sections offer email lists for discussion of relevant topics and events.

NLM has a variety of lists for announcements and discussions of their databases and resources. These include lists for announcement of new and updated NLM files and webpages, MedlinePlus topics, GoLocal, and PubMed. A full list is available at www.nlm.nih.gov/listserv/emaillists.html.

Other library-related lists that may be useful are:

- NGC4Lib, dewey.library.nd.edu/mailing-lists/ngc4lib: next-generation catalogs for libraries

- SLA-DSOL, units.sla.org/division/dsol/Discussion.html: SLA's solo librarians list, especially useful for hospital librarians

- SYSLIB-L, listserv.indiana.edu/cgi-bin/wa-iub.exe?A0=SYSLIB-L: an email list for systems librarians

- Web4Lib, lists.webjunction.org/web4lib: for discussion of library-based web servers and web design topics

Training

Anyone new to the field or interested in learning about health sciences librarianship will want to take advantage of training and education opportunities. The NN/LM offers a variety of free training resources. In addition to face-to-face classes and distance education courses, NN/LM also provides workbooks, tutorials, manuals, handouts, and presentations. Topics include consumer health, document delivery, PubMed, how to make a podcast, health literacy, technology trends, electronic resources, and many more. All of the NN/LM's educational resources are listed at nnlm.gov/training. The NN/LM's National Training Center and Clearinghouse (NTCC), headquartered at the New York Academy of Medicine, also provides free classes on PubMed, NLM Gateway, LinkOut, Molecular Biology, and the Unified Medical Language System. Information about NTCC classes can be found at nnlm. gov/ntcc. NTCC also maintains the Educational Clearinghouse, a database of "educational materials available to the public concerning biomedical and health related issues,"[6] located at nnlm.gov/ntcc/ch.

The Infopeople Project, administered by the California State Library and funded by the Institute of Museum and Library Services, provides training classes to California librarians for a small fee. While in-person classes are restricted to library and information professionals working in California, training materials such as slides and handouts, as well as archived webcasts and webinars, are available on the Infopeople site (www.infopeople. org/training/webcasts/list/archived) for anyone to view at no cost. Recent relevant webinars include:

- Finding Easy-to-Read and Multilingual Health Information for Your Patrons

- Understanding Health Literacy

- Health Information for Kids and Teens and Seniors

- I Don't Give Medical Advice; I Dispense Quality Health Information

- Beyond MedlinePlus: Resources That Answer Those Other Tough Health Reference Questions

In addition to health information, other Infopeople continuing education topics that might be of interest are leadership and management, using various software and technologies, and public services.

Kovacs Consulting (www.kovacs.com) also provides fee-based online and in-person training and continuing education courses for librarians. Courses can be scheduled through library associations or for individuals. Current topics include:

- Health and Medical Reference on the Web for Health Professionals and Researchers

- Evaluating Medical Information on the Web

- Health and Medical Reference on the Web for Healthcare Consumers

- How to Find Good CAM (Complementary and Alternative Medical) Information on the Web

- Electronic Collection Development for Health and
  Medicine E-Libraries

All of these courses are approved for MLA continuing education credits, which can be useful when applying for the Academy of Health Information Professionals (or AHIP, described in the next section).

The MLA regularly offers distance education teleconferences. Topics run the gamut, from licensing electronic content to emerging technologies to marketing and promoting the library. These teleconferences are broadcast via satellite at health sciences libraries across the country. Libraries that host these teleconferences generally post announcements to library lists publicizing the event for anyone interested in attending. For those unable to see the live teleconference, MLA has videos and DVDs for purchase. MLA maintains a list of distance education teleconferences at www.mlanet.org/education/telecon.

If you decide to join the health sciences library profession, there are also training opportunities designed to help you advance in the field. One such program is the NLM and Association of Academic Health Sciences Libraries' Leadership Fellows Program, designed to develop future library leaders. To apply for this competitive yearlong program, you must have a minimum of five years as a department head and a desire to become a library director.[7] Another example is NLM's BioMedical Informatics Course, held at Woods Hole, Massachusetts. This program uses a combination of lectures and hands-on exercises to introduce the "conceptual and technical components of medical informatics."[8] Directed at medical educators, librarians, administrators, and faculty, this weeklong course is taught by nationally recognized and respected faculty. These are just two examples of the types of opportunities that exist for health sciences librarians to take their career to a new level.

Credentialing

If you have browsed through job ads for medical/health sciences librarians, you have probably noticed the phrase "AHIP required or preferred." Created in 1989, AHIP is MLA's "peer-reviewed professional development and career recognition program"[9] (MLA had earlier credentialing programs as far back as 1949[10]). For the history of, revisions to, and the debate behind MLA's credentialing efforts, Jo Ann H. Bell's article "History of the Medical Library Association's Credentialing Program" is the best starting point. The current program is designed to recognize librarians' efforts, achievements, and service within their role as a health sciences information professional and focuses on continuing professional development.

Admission to AHIP centers around three broad categories: academic preparation, professional experience, and professional accomplishments documented in a portfolio. The portfolio consists of a series of forms, depending on the level at which you are applying and whether you hold an ALA-accredited degree, and the level depends on your amount of time in the profession. For instance, the provisional level is for people with five or fewer years of experience, the member and senior levels require more than five years, and applying at the distinguished level requires 10 or more years of experience. Once accepted, you will need to renew your membership every five years at the current fee (right now $100 for provisional status and $175 for other levels). The AHIP website (www.mlanet.org/academy) has all sorts of information including FAQs, Hints for a Successful Portfolio, and all the forms needed to complete your portfolio.

In our survey, 347 people responded to the question "What is your AHIP status?" Of those, 124 (35.7 percent) did have AHIP status, while 223 (64.3 percent) did not have AHIP status. Among those who did have status, 4.6 percent were at provisional level, 6.3 percent were at member level, 7.5 percent were at senior level, 16.1

percent were at distinguished level, and 1.2 percent had emeritus status. Among those who were not AHIP members, 6.6 percent said that AHIP was not applicable while 57.6 percent indicated they were not members. This response raised some questions. Since the majority of responding AHIP members were at the senior or distinguished level, it's possible that new health sciences librarians aren't interested in credentialing—but perhaps people are just waiting until they have more time in the field before applying. Bell explains that proponents of the program see it as way to gain status for the profession and encourage continued education and growth, while the program's critics argue that no one program can truly reflect the diversity of what health sciences librarians do and that the requirements are not universally recognized and are unlikely to result in any status gain. Some even argue that the requirements are so easy that the membership is meaningless.[11]

Luckily, you can apply for AHIP status at any time. If you are unsure whether you want to continue working in health sciences librarianship or if AHIP is right for your situation, you do not have to apply right away. Just keep an ongoing track of the documentation AHIP requires you to submit in case you decide to pursue AHIP later, choose to look for another health sciences librarian position, or need to apply for status to advance (either in position or rank) in your current job.

Along the same lines, make sure to review MLA's list of professional competencies for health sciences librarians (www.mlanet.org/education/policy/executive_summary.html#B) to ensure that the requirements are met either through academic coursework or through continuing education coursework. When applying for AHIP membership, applicants have to document instruction in each of the competencies. Also take a look at "Health Sciences Information Knowledge and Skills" (www.mlanet.org/education/policy/knowledge.html), which provides further details and examples for each of these competencies.

Peers

Finally, don't forget your peers. Your fellow health sciences librarians are your greatest resource. New health sciences librarians should find mentors in a couple of veteran health sciences librarians to help you learn not only the resources but also the environment and politics of health sciences librarianship (they'll prove to be good references, too). You can find a good mentor most anywhere. MLA does offer some programs, like AHIP, that require you to draw from a designated pool of people. But don't let that stop you from finding your own mentors as you lurk on lists and participate in meetings and conferences. In many cases, your "unofficial" mentors are the most valuable. Also, there usually isn't one person that can serve all your mentoring needs.

Where To Go From Here

While this book doesn't tell you everything you will ever need to know about health sciences librarianship, it will hopefully give you a place to start if you find that you've become an accidental health sciences librarian or if you are curious and considering entering the health sciences library niche. If you are still in school, our best advice is to take a medical library related course and to do an internship or practicum in a health sciences library. An internship or practicum is one of the best ways to get a real look inside. Together we've done either practica, internships, or student work in a law library, map library, special collections, and general academic as well as health sciences libraries, and those experiences were worth their weight in gold.

We've tried to show throughout this book that, while health sciences has a lot in common with its library siblings, there is a good bit that is different and unique. We've also tried to make sure we've listed a good number of resources on topics such as licensing and collection development—which could easily warrant their own book! We also hope we've shown health sciences librarianship in an accurate light. It isn't for everyone, and there are definitely some frustrations unique to the field. But for those who do find a home in health sciences librarianship, the potential rewards are also unique. The following responses from the survey illustrate some of these rewards:

- "The field of medicine. It is so fascinating. I learn something new every day. I also find value in knowing I have a direct impact on a person's health by providing and making available information to the healthcare professional."

- "Every day I make a difference in the lives of individuals, directly or indirectly, by working with health professionals, health sciences students, and the larger community. I'm constantly challenged to become better at reference, information seeking, and evaluating the ever-growing medical literature."

- "Helping nursing students and faculty in their search for information, and incorporating critical thinking skills in this, leading to evidence-based practice. It is inspiring to be able to contribute to the care of patients through my work with nursing students and faculty."

- "The immediate gratification of knowing I am doing something useful and in real time to help patients. Reference at a university felt more removed from real life—the contribution to society much harder to trace. I also enjoy the challenge of searching for medical information."

- "I believe that medical librarians can literally 'help save lives' in doing urgent patient care literature searches. Finding evidence-based literature helps in physicians' and other healthcare workers' decision making. I also love to do consumer health searches for patients and families. I truly believe that 'knowledge is power' when it comes to having good evidence-based literature to aid in healthcare decision making."

- "Everything! I have the opportunity to touch so many lives every day, by offering information from a number of resources to patients, family members, and employees, which helps them to make wise healthcare decisions and reinforces their ability to ask appropriate questions regarding their care."

We are maintaining a blog with links to the resources in the book, as well as new stuff as we find it, at ahslbook.wordpress.com. We'd love to hear from you, so feel free to contact us through the blog or email us at ahslbook@gmail.com.

Endnotes

1. Medical Library Association homepage, www.mlanet.org

2. MLA Section Council, "Special Interest Group Manual," scouncil. mlanet.org/blogs/sigs/sigmanual

3. Journal of Consumer Health on the Internet, "Aim & Scope," www.informaworld.com/smpp/title~db=all~content=t792303980~tab =summary

4. Medical Library Association, "MEDLIB-L: An Email List for Medical Librarians," www.mlanet.org/discussion/medlibl.html

5. Medical Library Association, "Email Discussion Lists," www.mlanet. org/discussion

6. National Network of Libraries of Medicine, "Educational Clearinghouse Database: Search," nnlm.gov/ntcc/ch

7. Association of Academic Health Sciences Libraries, "NLM/AAHSL Leadership Fellows Program," aahsl.org/Applications_Awards_ Scholarships/NLM_AAHSL2008-2009rev.pdf

8. BioMedical Informatics, "BioMedical Informatics Course Overview," courses.mbl.edu/mi

9. Medical Library Association, "The Academy of Health Information Professionals," www.mlanet.org/academy

10. Jo Ann H. Bell, "History of the Medical Library Association's Credentialing Program," *Bulletin of the Medical Library Association* 84, no. 3 (July 1996): 320.

11. Bell, "History of the Medical Library Association's Credentialing Program," 330.

Appendix A

The Accidental Health Sciences Librarian Survey

This informal survey was posted as an online form from March to April 2008. Announcements were posted to various lists, including MEDLIB-L and Medical Library Association (MLA) chapter lists, as well as some nonmedical lists like NEWLIB-L, SYSLIB-L, and AUTOCAT. More than 300 people responded to the survey, including public, academic, hospital, and Area Health Education Centers (AHEC) librarians, as well as those working in government agency libraries, association and society libraries, and corporate libraries. All responses were kept anonymous.

The Accidental Health Sciences Librarian

Calling *all* health sciences, biomedical, and science librarians! Please take a few moments to complete the AHSL survey!

With the current emphasis on patient empowerment, as well as the plethora of all sorts of different health sciences programs in a variety of settings, from two year colleges to research universities, *The Accidental Health Sciences Librarian*, forthcoming from Information Today, Inc., will serve as a valuable resource for both new and veteran librarians, no matter the type or size of the library. There is the potential for any librarian to encounter a health sciences question or issue, whether it be from a doctor attempting to treat a patient, a student from a local nursing program, a lawyer researching a case, or a public library patron looking for drug or health information. Health sciences librarianship is a dynamic and challenging field that offers librarians a unique opportunity to make an immediate impact. Overall, the purpose of the book is to give those librarians who have found themselves unexpectedly navigating the maze of health sciences information the confidence and knowledge to cope with any situation that should arise.

Lisa and Nicole thank you in advance for your participation in the survey. It should take about 10 minutes to complete. If you have any questions or comments, please don't hesitate to contact the authors at ahslbook@gmail.com.

1. What is your job title?

2. What is your AHIP status?

   - Provisional

   - Member

   - Senior

   - Distinguished

   - Emeritus

   - Not a member

3. To which library associations/organizations do you belong? Which are your favorite and why?

4. In what type of library do you work?

   - Academic

   - Hospital

   - Public

   - AHEC

   - Other (please specify)

5. What is your age range?

   - 20–29

   - 30–39

   - 40–49

   - 50+

6. In what region do you live?

   - Middle Atlantic (Delaware, New Jersey, New York, Pennsylvania)

   - Southeastern Atlantic (Alabama, District of Columbia, Florida, Georgia, Maryland, Mississippi, North Carolina, Puerto Rico, South Carolina, Tennessee, Virginia, West Virginia, U.S. Virgin Islands)

   - Greater Midwest (Illinois, Indiana, Iowa, Kentucky, Michigan, Minnesota, North Dakota, Ohio, South Dakota, Wisconsin)

   - Midcontinental (Colorado, Kansas, Missouri, Nebraska, Utah, Wyoming)

   - South Central (Arkansas, Louisiana, New Mexico, Oklahoma, Texas)

   - Pacific Northwest (Alaska, Idaho, Montana, Oregon, Washington)

   - Pacific Southwest (Arizona, California, Hawaii, Nevada, Pacific Basin)

   - New England (Connecticut, Maine, Massachusetts, New Hampshire, Rhode Island, Vermont)

   - Other (please specify)

7. From what ALA accredited program did you receive your library degree?

8. Did you take a health sciences course in library school?

- Yes

- No, because my program did *not* offer a course in health sciences librarianship.

- No, I chose not to take the health sciences course.

- No, I wanted to take the course but it didn't fit my schedule.

- Other (please specify)

9. What other degrees do you hold? Please list all degrees, fields, and schools (ex: MA History, State U).

10. Please describe your path to health sciences librarianship.

11. What do you love about being a health sciences librarian?

12. What are your *least* favorite things about being in health sciences librarianship?

13. What are the greatest challenges in health sciences librarianship today?

14. Why should librarians choose health sciences librarianship over other types of librarianship?

15. How do you keep current in the profession? What blogs, wikis, listservs, journals, or other resources do you read?

16. What advice would you give someone who is interested in health sciences librarianship?

17. How did you hear about this survey?

18. Any additional comments or thoughts?

19. Are you willing to talk further with the authors? If so, please include your contact information in the box below. (All data will be kept confidential.)

Selected Responses to Survey Questions

Selected Responses to "What Do You Love About Being a Health Sciences Librarian?"

"Knowing that I'm helping with the education of medical students, residents, faculty, staff, and the general public. Also, having an indirect (and sometimes direct) influence on patient care." —Academic Librarian

"The information sought will be used to improve someone's health or empower their decisions regarding their health." —Academic Librarian

"The challenges, you are never bored working in an HS library." —Academic Librarian

"The challenge of never knowing quite what kind of questions/issues you will be faced with daily and the fact that you are always helping someone." —Academic Librarian

"Participating in the healthcare process, feeling like I am contributing positively to patient care, working collaboratively with health care professionals." —Academic Librarian

"Helping nursing students and faculty in their search for information, and incorporating critical thinking skills in this, leading to evidence-based practice. It is inspiring to be able to contribute to the care of patients through my work with nursing students and faculty." —Academic Librarian

"I like working with the variety of users we have, from faculty to students to clinicians. I love helping people find information and doing searches for busy clinicians. I love being able to provide resources that our users find useful." —Academic Librarian

"I've always been very interested in health-related topics but could never settle on just one area. I love the variety of health topics I get to learn about during my work. I feel like the health librarians are ahead of the curve in terms of technology and controlled vocabulary. I like the fast-paced nature of it. I also like being able to help friends and family find information whenever they have a health issue." —Academic Librarian

"Being in the forefront of introducing health information that affects management's and clinicians' decision making." —Hospital Librarian

"Utter variety in the levels of information needs, from patients to nurses to administrators to physicians." —Hospital Librarian

"The newness, every day, and the chance to participate with, and give help to, the myriad information seekers, from professional to patient, that we meet every day." —Hospital Librarian

"Hearing the feedback. Not often, but occasionally, I do hear, and it is very rewarding to hear that a patient survived, or made it into a clinical trial, or their baby will grow up to be normal." —Hospital Librarian

"The ability to make a visible, long-lasting impact on people's health, quality of life, and empowerment. Patients have told me that they received more information from me than their providers, and because of it they were able to make informed decisions and influence their own care. Providers tell us that our services change the way they treat patients and impact the fiscal bottom line by enabling the right testing/treatment the first time around." —Hospital Librarian

"Being able to help people with their information needs that really affect their lives and their well-being. Being able to help reassure and relieve confusion about their health issues." —Public Librarian

"Empowering people through information and reducing their anxiety." —Public Librarian

"Helping medical professionals and laypeople with info needs; learning about medicine on a daily basis." —AHEC Librarian

"Complexity and variations in questions." —AHEC Librarian

"I love doing the searches for the information the medical professionals need. There's always that thrill when I find 'just the right' source." —Corporate Research Librarian

"I really like the medical/health part. Sometimes wish I had majored in biology and become a doctor (or veterinarian) but it's too late for that now—so being a medical librarian lets me work in the health/medical field." —Professional Association Librarian

"Being immersed in the latest research news for health and medicine, which is personally fascinating, but more importantly, fulfills the public's needs for reliable and current health guidance. Having powerful information tools at my fingertips to search for basic information/sources, or to hunt down the more elusive quarry, is perfect." —Federal Librarian

Selected Responses to "What Are Your *Least* Favorite Things About Being in Health Sciences Librarianship?"

"Outrageous costs set by publishers." —Academic Librarian

"Dealing with overly confident medical students and residents." —Academic Librarian

"Working so fast, keeping up with the plethora of new information tools, and critical nature of the work." —Academic Librarian

"The frustration I feel when I cannot find the information needed, particularly when it is for a patient. I also don't appreciate when patrons believe I should be able to give them exactly what they want without being able to take a few minutes to conduct a reference interview; I know they are busy, but I won't be of much help if I don't know what they need!" —Academic Librarian

"Constant battle to justify our existence/funding shortfalls." —Academic Librarian

"Trying to get room in the medical school curriculum to teach skills these folks really, really need." —Academic Librarian

"Lack of recognition of importance of information to quality care among administrators." —Academic Librarian

"Change, specifically in terms of technology, happens so rapidly it can be very difficult to keep up. Often, I wonder if librarians are sacrificing patron service at the expense of providing the latest technological advances." —Academic Librarian

"The assumption that anyone can do what we do because of the ubiquity of information on the internet." —Academic Librarian

"Can be too stodgy. Folks need to loosen up a bit." —Academic Librarian

"Not a typical day at the office—unpredictable circumstances prevent me from getting things done." —Hospital Librarian

"Uncertainty about funding and being gouged by publishers." —Hospital Librarian

"Everyone wants the information yesterday! Doctors are always in a rush and they don't want to do searches, etc., themselves." —Hospital Librarian

"Worrying about the budget and which journals or books that I might have to cut due to budget constraints." —Hospital Librarian

"Finding information for a parent that their child's illness is fatal (when they didn't already know that)." —Hospital Librarian

"Being crushed under the weight of the bureaucracy. Bad side of working for a large organization, trying to get the battleship to move faster and also having to get buy-in from so many other stakeholders." —Hospital Librarian

"Trying to prove our value and the high cost of offering good service." —Hospital Librarian

"Full-color images of things I'd rather not see!" —Hospital Librarian

"Dealing with patients who have a debilitating condition—it is heartbreaking." —Hospital Librarian

"Sometimes it is very stressful. In addition, being a librarian in a corporation dominated by health care professionals can be frustrating as they often don't understand my role." —Hospital Librarian

"People needing more help than I can give." —Public Librarian

"Not being sure of the latest information." —Public Librarian

"Outmoded attitudes toward technology among many of my peers." —AHEC Librarian

"No one knows what a medical librarian does." —Society Librarian

Selected Responses to "What Are the Greatest Challenges in Health Sciences Librarianship Today?"

"Simply surviving." —Academic Librarian

"Shifting to provide more nontraditional services (patient education committee, safety committee, evidence-based practice, knowledge management ... depends on the specific organization; moving away from database searching and into answering the question, not providing a list of possible articles." —Academic Librarian

"1. Trying to get a handle on the overload of medical information and making it easily available to your patrons. 2. Educating patrons about the many library resources available that continually change. 3. Keeping up with what I need to know." —Academic Librarian

"Getting young students interested in the field." —Academic Librarian

"Communicating, reaching out to nonusers and users, making sure electronic resources are available remotely and that users know how to get to them easily, being able to afford to provide resources, competing with Google, and other non-librarian produced resources that could pretty easily be seen and used as replacements to us." —Academic Librarian

"Defining roles and integrating into a variety of hot-button issues in health sciences education: curriculum development, EMR evaluation and integration, involvement in EBM training." —Academic Librarian

"Proving the library's worth in the community hospital setting." —Academic Librarian

"Defining and redefining what our roles are and what they can be. Also, figuring out how to do it all and not be stressed all the time. Figuring out how to be respected and compensated for what we as information professionals bring to the education and healthcare systems." —Academic Librarian

"Advocacy. We need to constantly tell administrators that what we do is mission critical and essential to quality patient care and economically sound. Without this understanding, more administrators will continue to think that everything is available on the web or a librarian can be replaced with one database." —Academic Librarian

"Closing of libraries." —Hospital Librarian

"Embracing 'Evidence-based Information & Librarianship.'" —Hospital Librarian

"Staying on top of the technology and remaining visible and valid enough to stay open." —Hospital Librarian

"Becoming analyzers, interpreters and synthesizers of information for busy clinicians." —Hospital Librarian

"Learning to think outside of the box." —Hospital Librarian

"Competition from businesses/publishers, falling behind in technology, state of healthcare industry, where shortage of money may mean an extinction of the libraries." —Hospital Librarian

"The ethical lines between giving information and giving advice." —Public Librarian

"Keeping up with the latest research." —Public Librarian

"Bringing in new grads." —AHEC Librarian

"We have to move into a new universe of information, and the old ways of delivering information to users need to be rethought." —AHEC Librarian

"Survival as a profession." —Government Research Librarian

Selected Health Sciences Library Associations

Medical Library Association (www.mlanet.org)

Chapters

Hawaii-Pacific Chapter, hpcmla.mlanet.org

Medical Library Group of Southern California and Arizona, www.mlgsca.mlanet.org

Mid-Atlantic Chapter, macmla.org

Midcontinental Chapter, www.mcmla.org

Midwest Chapter, midwestmla.org

New York-New Jersey Chapter, www.nynjmla.org

North Atlantic Health Sciences Libraries, www.nahsl.org

Northern California and Nevada Medical Library Group, ncnmlg.stanford.edu

Pacific Northwest Chapter, depts.washington.edu/pncmla

Philadelphia Regional Chapter, www.mlaphil.org

South Central Chapter, www.sccmla.org

Southern Chapter, www.scmla.org

Upstate New York and Ontario Chapter, unyoc.mlanet.org

Sections

Cancer Librarians Section, www.selu.com/cancerlib

Chiropractic Libraries Section, www.cls.mlanet.org

Collection Development Section, colldev.mlanet.org

Consumer and Patient Health Information Section, caphis.mlanet.org

Corporate Information Services Section, ciss.mlanet.org

Dental Section, mladentalsection.pbwiki.com

Educational Media and Technologies Section, emts.mlanet.org
Federal Libraries Section, fls.mlanet.org
Health Association Libraries Section, www.hals.mlanet.org
Hospital Libraries Section, www.hls.mlanet.org
International Cooperation Section, ics.mlanet.org
Leadership and Management Section,
    www.lms.mlanet.org/index.html
Medical Informatics Section, www.medinfo.mlanet.org
Medical Library Education Section, mles.mlanet.org
Nursing and Allied Health Resources Section, nahrs.mlanet.org
Pharmacy and Drug Information Section, www.pdi.mlanet.org
Public Health/Health Administration Section,
    www.phha.mlanet.org
Public Services Section, pss.mlanet.org
Relevant Issues Section, ri.mlanet.org
Research Section, research.mlanet.org
Technical Services Section, techservices.mlanet.org
Veterinary Medical Libraries Section, www.vmls.mlanet.org

Special Interest Groups (SIGs)
African-American Medical Librarians Alliance, aamla.mlanet.org
Clinical Librarians and Evidence-Based Health Care (no website)
Complementary and Alternative Medicine, camsig.mlanet.org
Department of the Army Medical Command Libraries (no
    website)
Department of Veterans Affairs Librarians (no website)
Institutional Animal Care and Use (no website)
Lesbian, Gay, Bisexual, and Transgendered Health Science
    Librarians, lgbt.mlanet.org
Libraries in Curriculum, groups.google.com/group/libraries-in-
    curriculum
Library Marketing, www.library-marketing-sig.mlanet.org
Mental Health, www.miami.edu/mhsig

Molecular Biology and Genomics (no website)
New Member, www.newmembers.mlanet.org
OCLC (no website)
Osteopathic Libraries, www.olsig.mlanet.org
Outreach, www.outreachsig.mlanet.org
Pediatric Libraries, pedsig.mlanet.org
Vision Science Librarians, ww.avsl.org
Voyager (no website)

State Associations

Alabama Health Libraries Association,
    southmed.usouthal.edu/library/alhela
Arizona [Central] Biomedical Libraries, www.samaritan.edu/cabl
Colorado Council of Medical Librarians, www.ccmlnet.org
Connecticut Association of Health Sciences Librarians,
    library.umassmed.edu/cahsl
District of Columbia Area Health Sciences Libraries,
    www8.georgetown.edu/dml/dcahsl
Florida Health Sciences Library Association, www.fhsla.org
Georgia Health Sciences Library Association, www.ghsla.org
Idaho's Medical Libraries, ihia.lili.org
Illinois [Health Sciences Librarians of], hsli.org
Indiana Health Sciences Librarians Association,
    www.incolsa.net/~ihsla
Iowa Health Sciences Library Association,
    hosted.lib.uiowa.edu/hsround
Kentucky Medical Library Association, library.sullivan.edu/kmla
Louisiana [Health Sciences Library Association of], www.hslal.org
Maine Health Science Libraries and Information Consortium,
    library.umassmed.edu/hslic
Maryland Association of Health Sciences Librarians,
    www.mahsl.umaryland.edu

Massachusetts Health Sciences Library Network,
www.mahslin.org

Michigan Health Sciences Libraries Association, www.mhsla.org

Minnesota [Health Sciences Libraries of],
blog.lib.umn.edu/lmcguire/hslm

Missouri [Health Sciences Library Network-Kansas City],
www.hslnkc.org

Nebraska ICON Library Consortium, www.iconlibrary.org

New Hampshire [The Health Science Libraries of New Hampshire
and Vermont], library.umassmed.edu/hslnhvt

New Jersey [Health Sciences Library Association of],
www.hslanj.org

North Carolina [Association of North Carolina Health and Science
Libraries], www.anchasl.org

Ohio Health Sciences Library Association, www.ohslanet.org

Oklahoma Health Sciences Library Association,
library.ouhsc.edu/ohsla.cfm

Oregon Health Sciences Libraries Association,
www.ohsu.edu/library/ohsla

Pennsylvania [Central] Health Sciences Library Association,
www.cphsla.org

Rhode Island [Association of Rhode Island Health Sciences
Libraries], library.umassmed.edu/arihsl

Tennessee Health Science Library Association,
www.tha.com/all_aff/thesla.htm

Texas Health Sciences Libraries Consortium, ils.mdacc.tmc.edu

Utah Health Sciences Library Consortium,
library.med.utah.edu/uhslc

Vermont [The Health Science Libraries of New Hampshire and
Vermont], library.umassmed.edu/hslnhvt

Washington Medical Librarians Association, www.wmla.org

Wisconsin Health Science Library Association,
www.whsla.mcw.edu

Appendix D

Selected Health Sciences Organizations

Agency for Healthcare Research and Quality, www.ahrq.gov

American Association of Colleges of Nursing, www.aacn.nche.edu

American Association of Colleges of Pharmacy, www.aacp.org

American Association for Health Education,
www.aahperd.org/AAHE

American Association for the History of Medicine,
www.histmed.org

American Association for Respiratory Care, www.aarc.org

American College of Sports Medicine, www.acsm.org

American Dental Association, www.ada.org

American Dental Education Association, www.adea.org

American Dietetic Association, www.eatright.org

American Health Information Management Association,
www.ahima.org

American Hospital Association, www.aha.org

American Medical Association, www.ama-assn.org

American Medical Informatics Association, www.amia.org

American Nurses Association, www.nursingworld.org

American Nursing Informatics Association, www.ania.org

American Occupational Therapy Association, www.aota.org

American Pharmacists Association, www.pharmacist.com

American Physical Therapy Association, www.apta.org

American Public Health Association, www.apha.org

American Society for Clinical Laboratory Science, www.ascls.org

Archivists and Librarians in the History of the Health Sciences,
www.alhhs.org

Association of Academic Health Centers, www.aahcdc.org

Association of Academic Health Sciences Libraries,
www.aahsl.org

Association of American Medical Colleges, www.aamc.org

Association of Faculties of Medicine of Canada, www.afmc.ca

Association of Schools and Colleges of Optometry,
www.opted.org

Association of Vision Science Librarians, www.avsl.org

Centre for Evidence Based Medicine, www.cebm.net

Health on the Net Foundation, www.hon.ch

Health and Science Communications Association, www.hesca.org

Institute of Medicine, www.iom.edu

Interagency Council on Information Resources in Nursing,
www.icirn.org

Joint Commission (formerly Joint Commission on Accreditation
of Healthcare Organizations), www.jointcommission.org

Libraries in Medical Education,
www.aahsl.org/mc/page.do?sitePageId=84885

National Area Health Education Center Organization,
www.nationalahec.org

National Athletic Trainers' Association, www.nata.org

National Center for Health Statistics, www.cdc.gov/nchs

National Institutes of Health, www.nih.gov

National Library of Medicine, www.nlm.nih.gov

Partners in Information Access for the Public Health Workforce,
phpartners.org

Radiological Society of North America, www.rsna.org

U.S. Department of Health and Human Services, www.hhs.gov

World Health Organization, www.who.int/en

Recommended Reading

Chapter 1: Health Sciences Librarianship

Braude, Robert M. "On the Origin of a Species: Evolution of Health Sciences Librarianship." *Bulletin of the Medical Library Association* 85, no. 1 (Jan. 1997): 1–10.

Cheshier, Robert G. *Principles of Medical Librarianship: The Environment Affecting Health Sciences Libraries.* Cleveland, OH: Cleveland Health Sciences Library, 1975.

Gartland, Henry J. "The Veterans Administration Library Program." *Bulletin of the Medical Library Association* 56, no. 1 (Jan. 1968): 21–23.

Irish, D. Elizabeth, and Susan E. Lahey. "What's Your Verdict? A Unique Way to Introduce MLS Students to Health Sciences Librarianship." *Journal of Hospital Librarianship* 1, no. 1 (2001): 139–141.

Lynch, Jill Anne. "Providing Library Services to Deployed Army Medical Providers in Iraq and Afghanistan." *Journal of Hospital Librarianship* 8, no. 2 (May 2008): 218–229.

McClure, Lucretia. *Health Sciences Environment and Librarianship in Health Sciences Libraries.* New York: Forbes Custom Publishing, 1999.

Medical Library Association. "Join the Health Care Team: Become a Medical Librarian." Video. www.mlanet.org/career/career_vid.html

Medical Library Association. "Medical Librarianship: A Career Beyond the Cutting Edge." Presentation. www.mlanet.org/ppt/career/cutting_edge_english_new.ppt

Preddie, Martha I. "The Lone Ranger Part I: Charting New Grounds in Prison Hospital Librarianship." *Journal of Hospital Librarianship* 6, no. 1 (2006): 87–93.

Van Vuren, Darcy D. "The Veterans Administration Library Network: VALNET." *Bulletin of the Medical Library Association* 70, no. 3 (July 1982): 289–292.

Chapter 2: Putting the Medical in Health Sciences Librarianship

Bachrach, C. A., and Thelma Charen. "Selection of MEDLINE Contents, the Development of Its Thesaurus, and the Indexing Process." *Med Inform* 3, no. 3 (Sept. 1978): 237–254.

Bunting, Alison. *The Nation's Health Information Network: History of the Regional Medical Library Program, 1965–1985.* Chicago: MLA, 1987.

Chapman, Carleton B. *Order Out of Chaos: John Shaw Billings and America's Coming of Age.* Boston: Boston Medical Library, 1994.

Chilov, Marina, Konstantina Matsoukas, Nighat Ispahany, Tracy Y. Allen, and Joyce W. Lustbader. "Using MeSH to Search for Alternatives to the Use of Animals in Research." *Medical Reference Services Quarterly* 26, no. 3 (Fall 2007): 55–73.

Garrison, Fielding H., and Adelaide Hasse. *John Shaw Billings: A Memoir.* New York: G.P. Putnam's Sons, 1915.

Miles, Wyndham D. *A History of the National Library of Medicine: The Nation's Treasury of Medical Knowledge.* Washington, DC: Government Printing Office, 1982. www.nlm.nih.gov/hmd/manuscripts/miles/miles.html

National Library of Medicine. "Fact Sheet: Medical Subject Headings (MeSH)." www.nlm.nih.gov/pubs/factsheets/mesh.html

Rogers, Frank B. "The Development of MEDLARS." *Bulletin of the Medical Library Association* 52, no. 1 (Jan. 1964): 150–151.

Womack, Kristina R. "Conformity for Conformity's Sake? The Choice of a Classification System and a Subject Heading System in Academic Health Sciences Libraries." *Cataloging & Classification Quarterly* 42, no. 1 (2006): 93–115.

Chapter 3: It's All About the People

Albert, Karen M. "Integrating Knowledge-Based Resources Into the Electronic Health Record: History, Current Status, and Role of Librarians." *Medical Reference Services Quarterly* 26, no. 3 (Fall 2007): 1–19.

Allcock, J. "Helping Public Library Patrons Find Medical Information—The Reference Interview." *Public Library Quarterly* 18, nos. 3/4 (2000): 21–27.

Bennett-McNew, Christina, and Bart Ragon. "Inspiring Vanguards: The Woods Hole Experience." *Medical Reference Services Quarterly* 27, no. 1 (Spring 2008): 105–110.

Bridges, Jane, Christian J. Miller, and Daniel G. Kipnis. "Librarians in the Woods Hole Biomedical Informatics Course." *Medical Reference Services Quarterly* 25, no. 1 (Spring 2006): 71–81.

Campbell, Jayne M., and Nancy K. Roderer. "Fellowship Training at Johns Hopkins: Programs Leading to Careers in Librarianship and Informatics as Informaticians or Informationists." *Medical Reference Services Quarterly* 24, no. 1 (Spring 2005): 93–99.

Cleveland, Ana D., and Donald B. Cleveland. *Health Informatics for Medical Librarians*. New York: Neal-Schuman, 2008.

Connor, Elizabeth. *A Guide to Developing End User Education Programs in Medical Libraries*. New York: Haworth Press, 2005.

Dorrington, Linda. "Health Libraries as Joint Use Libraries: Serving Medical Practitioners and Students." *Library Trends* 54, no. 4 (Spring 2006): 596–606.

Eberle, Michelle L. "Librarians' Perceptions of the Reference Interview." *Journal of Hospital Librarianship* 5, no. 3 (2005): 29–41.

Ellero, Nadine P. "Crossing Over: Health Sciences Librarians Contributing and Collaborating on Electronic Medical Record (EMR) Implementation." *Journal of Hospital Librarianship* 9, no. 1 (Jan. 2009): 89–107.

"Emerging Roles of Health Sciences Librarians, Part 1." *Reference Services Review* [special issue] 32, no. 1 (2004).

"Emerging Roles of Health Sciences Librarians, Part 2." *Reference Services Review* [special issue] 33, no. 1 (2005).

Geer, Renata C. "Broad Issues to Consider for Library Involvement in Bioinformatics." *Journal of the Medical Library Association* 94, no. 3 (July 2006): 286–298.

Giuse, Nunzia B., Taneya Y. Koonce, Rebecca N. Jerome, Molynda Cahall, Nila A. Sathe, and Annette Williams. "Evolution of a Mature Clinical Informationist Model." *Journal of the American Medical Informatics Association* 12, no. 3 (May/June 2005): 249–255.

Greenwood, Nancy, and Laurie Cole. "Supporting Consumer Health: A Hospital Library's Experience in Developing a Nursing Portal." *Journal of Hospital Librarianship* 9, no. 1 (Jan. 2009): 50–58.

Guessferd, Mimi. "The Clinical Librarian/Informationist: Past, Present, Future." *Journal of Hospital Librarianship* 6, no. 2 (2006): 65–73.

Harris, Martha R. "The Librarian's Roles in the Systematic Review Process: A Case Study." *Journal of the Medical Library Association* 93, no. 1 (Jan. 2005): 81–87.

Healy, Annette M. "MedlinePlus Go Local: The Librarian's Tool for Promoting Hospital Services to the Community." *Journal of Hospital Librarianship* 8, no. 3 (Aug. 2008): 344–351.

Hill, Thomas. "Fear, Concern, Fate, and Hope: Survival of Hospital Libraries." *Journal of the Medical Library Association* 95, no. 4 (Oct. 2007): 371–373.

Jones, Dee, and Donna F. Timm. "Consumer Health Search Engines Comparison." *Journal of Hospital Librarianship* 8, no. 4 (2008): 418–432.

Kane, Laura Townsend, Rozalynd P. McConnaugh, Steven Patrick Wilson, and David L. Townsend. *Answers to the Health Questions People Ask in Libraries.* New York: Neal-Schuman, 2008.

Kars, Marge, Lynda M. Baker, and Feleta Wilson., eds. *The Medical Library Association Guide to Health Literacy at the Library.* New York: Neal-Schuman, 2008.

Kash-Holley, Melissa J. "Development of a Patient and Visitor Information Kiosk." *Journal of Hospital Librarianship* 8, no. 4 (Nov. 2008): 449–456.

Kouame, Gail, Margo Harris, and Susan Murray. "Consumer Health Information From Both Sides of the Reference Desk." *Library Trends* 53, no. 3 (Winter 2005): 464–479.

Kovacs, Diane K. "Why Develop Web-Based Health Information Workshops for Consumers?" *Library Trends* 53, no. 2 (Fall 2004): 348–359.

Lacroix, Eve-Marie, and Joyce E. B. Backus. "Organizing Electronic Information to Serve the Needs of Health Practitioners and Consumers." *Library Trends* 54, no. 4 (Spring 2006): 607–619.

Lappa, Evagelia. "Clinical Librarianship (CL): A Historical Perspective." *Electronic Journal of Academic and Special Librarianship* 5, no. 2–3 (Fall 2004). southernlibrarianship.icaap. org/content/v05n02/lappa_e01.htm

Lewis, Deborah., ed. *Consumer Health Informatics: Informing Consumers and Improving Health Care.* New York: Springer, 2005.

Lyon, Jennifer A., Michele R. Tennant, Kevin R. Messner, and David L. Osterbur. "Carving a Niche: Establishing Bioinformatics Collaborations." *Journal of the Medical Library Association* 94, no. 3 (July 2006): 330–335.

Marshall, Joanne, Margaret Bandy, Kathy Lindner, Lisa McCormick, and Janet Schneider. "The Librarian's Role in the Provision of Consumer Health Information and Patient Education." *Bulleting of the Medical Library Association* 84, no. 2 (Apr. 1996): 238–239. caphis.mlanet.org/chis/librarian.html

McGowan, Jessie, and Margaret Sampson. "Systematic Reviews Need Systematic Searchers." *Journal of the Medical Library Association* 93, no. 1 (Jan. 2005): 74–80.

McKnight, Michelynn. "Librarians, Informaticists, Informationists, and Other Information Professionals in Biomedicine and the Health Sciences: What Do They Do?" *Journal of Hospital Librarianship* 5, no. 1 (2005): 13–29.

Medical Library Association. "Code of Ethics for Health Sciences Librarianship." 1994. www.mlanet.org/about/ethics.html

Medical Library Association. "Medical Library Association Policy Statement: The Role of Expert Searching in Health Sciences Libraries." 2003. www.mlanet.org/resources/expert_search/policy_expert_search.html

Minie, Mark, Stuart Bowers, Peter Tarczy-Hornoch, Edward Roberts, Rose A. James, Neil Rambo, and Sherrilynne Fuller. "The University of Washington Health Sciences Library BioCommons: An Evolving Northwest Biomedical Research Information Support Infrastructure." *Journal of the Medical Library Association* 94, no. 3 (July 2006): 321–329.

Morgan, Anna Beth Crabtree, and Holly E. Henderson. "Strengthening Consumer Health Information Delivery: An

Education and Promotion Project." *Journal of Hospital Librarianship* 6, no. 3 (2006): 1–17.

Murphy, Sarah Anne. "Consumer Health Information for Pet Owners." *Journal of the Medical Library Association* 94, no. 2 (Apr. 2006): 152–158.

Nicholson, Scott. "Understanding the Foundation: The State of Generalist Search Education in Library Schools as Related to the Needs of Expert Searchers in Medical Libraries." *Journal of the Medical Library Association* 93, no. 1 (Jan. 2005): 61–68.

Rein, Diane C. "Developing Library Bioinformatics Services in Context: The Purdue University Libraries Bioinformationist Program." *Journal of the Medical Library Association* 94, no. 3 (July 2006): 314–320.

Rios, Gabriel. "Creating a 'Virtual Expert' Presence in the Hospital Library." *Journal of Hospital Librarianship* 8, no. 4 (Nov. 2008): 457–463.

Ryan, Jeanette L. "AZHealthInfo: A Collaborative Model for Supporting the Health Information Needs of Public Health Workers, Public Librarians, Consumers, and Communities in Arizona." *Journal of the Medical Library Association* 95, no. 3 (Jul. 2007): 349–351.

Sewell, Robin R., Janis F. Brown, and Gale G. Hannigan. *Informatics in Health Sciences Curricula.* Chicago: Medical Library Association, 2005.

Snow, Bonnie. *Drug Information: A Guide to Current Resources.* New York: Neal-Schuman, 2008.

Spatz, Michele. *Answering Consumer Health Questions: The Medical Library Association Guide for Reference Librarians.* New York: Neal-Schuman, 2008.

Volk, Ruti Malis. "Expert Searching in Consumer Health: An Important Role for Librarians in the Age of the Internet and the Web." *Journal of the Medical Library Association* 95, no. 2 (Apr. 2007): 203–207.

Wilson, Jennifer Fisher. "Health Insurance Portability and
    Accountability Act Privacy Rule Causes Ongoing Concerns
    among Clinicians and Researchers." *Annals of Internal
    Medicine* 145, no. 4 (Aug. 2006): 313–316.

Wolf, Diane G., Christine C. Chastain-Warheit, Sharon Easterby-
    Gannett, Marion C. Chayes, and Bradley A. Long. "Hospital
    Librarianship in the United States: At the Crossroads." *Journal
    of the Medical Library Association* 90, no. 1 (Jan. 2002): 38–48.

Chapter 4: Technology

Bardyn, Tania, Caroline Young, and Lin C. Lombardi. "How We
    Surveyed Doctors to Learn What They Want From Computers
    and Technology." *Computers in Libraries* 28, no. 1 (Jan. 2008):
    7–11.

Boiko, Bob. *Laughing at the CIO: A Parable and Prescription for IT
    Leadership.* Medford, NJ: Information Today, Inc., 2007.

Boulos, Maged N. Kamel, Lee Hetherington, and Steve Wheeler.
    "Second Life: An Overview of the Potential of 3-D Virtual
    Worlds in Medical and Health Education." *Health Information
    and Libraries Journal* 24 (2007): 233–245.

Braun, Linda W. *Listen Up! Podcasting for Schools and Libraries.*
    Medford, NJ: Information Today, Inc., 2007.

Casey, Michael E., and Laura C. Savastinuk. *Library 2.0: A Guide to
    Participatory Library Service.* Medford, NJ: Information Today,
    Inc., 2007.

Craven, Jenny. *Web Accessibility: Practical Advice for the Library
    and Information Professional.* London: Facet Publishing, 2008.

Estabrook, Alexia D. "Leveraging Real Simple Syndication for
    Current Awareness." *Journal of Hospital Librarianship* 5, no. 3
    (2005): 83–92.

Ennis, Lisa A. "The Art of Talking Tech: Strategies for Effective
Communication With Information Technology Departments."
Journal of Hospital Librarianship 9, no. 2 (April 2009): 210–217.
———. "Talking the Talk: Communicating with IT." *Computers in
Libraries* 28, no. 8 (Sept. 2008): 14–18.

Farkas, Meredith G. *Social Software in Libraries: Building
Collaboration, Communication, and Community Online.*
Medford, NJ: Information Today, Inc., 2007.

Gordon, Rachel Singer. *The Accidental Systems Librarian.*
Medford, NJ: Information Today, Inc., 2003.

Kraft, Michelle A. "The Use of Blogs in Medical Libraries." *Journal
of Hospital Librarianship* 6, no. 1 (2006): 1–13.

Kroski, Ellyssa. *Web 2.0 for Librarians and Information
Professionals.* New York: Neal-Schuman, 2008.

Rethlefsen, Melissa L., Nicole C. Engard, Daphne Chang, and
Carol Haytko. "Social Software for Libraries and Librarians."
Journal of Hospital Librarianship 6, no. 4 (2006): 29–45.

Sauers, Michael P. *Blogging and RSS: A Librarian's Guide.*
Medford, NJ: Information Today, Inc., 2007.

Still, Julie M. *The Accidental Webmaster.* Medford, NJ: Information
Today, Inc., 2003.

Chapter 5: Databases and Resources

Albitz, Becky. *Licensing and Managing Electronic Resources.*
Oxford: Chandos Publishing, 2008.

Cuddy, Colleen. *Using PDAs in Libraries: A How-to-Do-It Manual.*
New York: Neal-Schuman, 2005.

Dee, Cheryl Rae. "The Development of the Medical Literature
Analysis and Retrieval System (MEDLARS)." *Journal of the
Medical Library Association* 95, no. 4 (Oct. 2007): 416–425.

Eames, Cathy H. "Circulating PDAs: A Hospital Library Experience." *Journal of Hospital Librarianship* 6, no. 1 (2006): 95–101.

Guenther, Kim. "Making Smart Licensing Decisions." *Computers in Libraries* 20, no. 6 (June 2000). www.infotoday.com/cilmag/jun00/guenther.htm

Harris, Lesley. "Deal-maker, Deal-breaker: When to Walk Away." *Library Journal* 125, no. 1 (Winter 2000): 12–14.

Harris, Lesley Ellen. *Licensing Digital Content: A Practical Guide for Librarians.* 2nd edition. Chicago: ALA Editions, 2009.

Katcher, Brian S. *MEDLINE: A Guide to Effective Searching in PubMed and Other Interfaces.* San Francisco: Ashbury Press, 2006.

Le Ber, Jeanne, Nancy Lombardo, John Bramble, and Deborah G. Lovett. "Medical Students Find Power in Their Palm: PDAs in a Clinical Rotation." *Journal of Electronic Resources in Medical Libraries* 2, no. 2 (2005): 91–100.

Pickett, Keith M. "Reading Beyond MEDLINE: A Beginner's Overview of Electronic Biomedical Resources." *Journal of Hospital Librarianship* 8, no. 4 (2008): 398–410.

Stave, Christopher D. *Field Guide to MEDLINE: Making Searching Simple.* Philadelphia: Lippincott Williams & Wilkins, 2003.

Chapter 6: Resources and Networking

Bell, Jo Ann H. "History of the Medical Library Association's Credentialing Program." *Bulletin of the Medical Library Association* 84, no.3 (July 1996): 320-333.

Chase, Darren. "Using Online Social Networks, Podcasting, and a Blog to Enhance Access to Stony Brook University Health Sciences Library Resources and Services." *Journal of Electronic Resources in Medical Libraries* 5, no. 2 (June 2008): 123–132.

Connor, Jennifer. *Guardians of Medical Knowledge: The Genesis of the Medical Library Association.* Lanham, MD: MLA and Scarecrow Press, 2000.

Darling, Louise. "The View Behind and Ahead: Implications of Certification." *Bulletin of the Medical Library Association* 61, no. 4 (Oct. 1973): 375–386.

Estabrook, Alexia D., and David L. Rothma. "Applications of RSS in Health Sciences Libraries." *Medical Reference Services Quarterly* 26, S1 (2007): 51–68.

Roper, Fred W. "The Medical Library Association's Professional Development Program: A Look Back at the Way Ahead." *Journal of the Medical Library Association* 94, no. 1 (Jan. 2006): 8–18.

Wu, Wendy G., and Jie Li. "RSS Made Easy." *Medical Reference Services Quarterly* 26, no. 1 (2006): 37–50.

Websites

Websites are listed by chapter in the order in which they appear. Updated links to these sites are available on the website for this book (ahslbook.wordpress.com).

Chapter 1: Health Sciences Librarianship

Knoxville Area Health Sciences Library Consortium, gsm.utmck.edu/library/kahslc/kahslc.htm

Lister Hill Library of the Health Sciences, University of Birmingham, www.uab.edu/lister

University of New Mexico Health Sciences Library and Informatics Center, hsc.unm.edu/library

Maguire Medical Library, Florida State University College of Medicine, www.med.fsu.edu/library

Sparks Medical Library, Huntsville Regional Medical Campus, University of Alabama School of Medicine, main.uab.edu/uasom/2/show.asp?durki=20025

Greenblatt Library, Medical College of Georgia, www.lib.mcg.edu

Mason Library, Keene State College, www.keene.edu/library

Ramsey Library, University of North Carolina at Asheville, www.lib.unca.edu/library

Georgia State University Library, www.library.gsu.edu

Galen College of Nursing, www.galened.com

New York University College of Dentistry, www.nyu.edu/dental

New England College of Optometry, www.neco.edu

David D. Palmer Health Sciences Library, College of Chiropractic, www.palmer.edu/libraryd.aspx

Veterinary Medical Libraries Section, Medical Library Association (MLA), www.vmls.mlanet.org

Veterinary Medical Libraries Section, Veterinary Medical and Related Libraries: An International Directory, www.vmls.mlanet.org/vlindex.htm

Pendergrass Agriculture & Veterinary Medicine Library, University of Tennessee at Knoxville, www.lib.utk.edu/agvet

Science Library, University of Georgia, www.libs.uga.edu/science

Gluck Equine Research Center Library, University of Kentucky, www.ca.uky.edu/gluck/ServLibrary.asp

Isabel McDonald Library, Oregon National Primate Research Center, www.ohsu.edu/library/primate.shtml

Zoological Society of San Diego Library, library.sandiegozoo.org

A. Carter Middendorf Library, Baltimore Aquarium, www.aqua.org

Directory of Zoo and Aquarium Libraries, www.nal.usda.gov/awic/zoo/ZooAquaLibDir.htm

National Zoological Park Branch Library, www.sil.si.edu/libraries/nzp

National Agricultural Library, U.S. Department of Agriculture, www.nal.usda.gov

Animal Welfare Information Center, awic.nal.usda.gov

AHEC Directory, www.nationalahec.org/Directory/AHEC Directory.asp

AHEC Libraries, University of Arkansas for Medical Sciences, www.uams.edu/AHEC/library.asp

Foothills AHEC Program, www.foothillsahec.org

North Carolina AHEC Information and Library System, library.ncahec.net/ILS

North Carolina AHEC Digital Library, library.ncahec.net

Joint Commission, www.jointcommission.org

Hospital Libraries Section, MLA, www.hls.mlanet.org/organization

Hospital Libraries Section Wiki, MLA, mla-hls.wikispaces.com

St. Luke's Cornwall Hospital, www.stlukescornwallhospital.org

St. Luke's Cornwall Hospital Library, www.slchlibrary.org

El Camino Hospital Health Library & Resource Center,
www.elcaminohospital.org/Patient_Services/Health_Library

Veteran Affairs (VA) Library Network, www1.va.gov/valnet

Michael E. DeBakey VA Medical Center's Patient Education
Resource Center, www.houston.va.gov/PatientEd/perc.asp

VA Long Beach Healthcare System,
www.longbeach.va.gov/Our_Services/library.asp

Vanderbilt University Medical Center Consumer Health Digital
Library, www.mc.vanderbilt.edu/vumcdiglib/subjres.html?
diglib=6

Consumer and Patient Health Information Section, MLA,
caphis.mlanet.org/consumer

National Network of Libraries of Medicine, nnlm.gov

Consumer Health Digital Library, Eskind Biomedical Library,
Vanderbilt Medical Center, www.mc.vanderbilt.edu/
vumcdiglib/subjres.html?diglib=6

Healthnet, University of Connecticut Health Center,
library.uchc.edu/departm/hnet/about.html

PlaneTree Health Library, www.planetreesanjose.org

Health & Education Resource Center, New York University (NYU),
www.nyupatientlibrary.org/cancer

Patient and Family Resource Center, NYU, www.nyupatient
library.org/medcenter

Family Health Resource Center & Patient Library, NYU, www.nyu
patientlibrary.org/hassenfeld

Mercer Medical Library and The Peyton T. Anderson Learning
Resources Center, medicine.mercer.edu/library_home

Learning Resource Center, Mayo Medical School,
www.mayo.edu/mms/learning-resource-center.html

History of Medicine Collection, National Library of Medicine,
    www.nlm.nih.gov/hmd
Reynolds Historical Library, University of Alabama at
    Birmingham, www.uab.edu/reynolds
Michigan State University Libraries Special Collections,
    spc.lib.msu.edu/html/materials/collections/vetmed_coll.jsp
History of the Health Sciences Section, MLA, www.mla-hhss.org

Chapter 2: Putting the Medical in Health Sciences Librarianship

National Library of Medicine (NLM), www.nlm.nih.gov
National Network of Libraries of Medicine (NN/LM), nnlm.gov
Armed Forces Medical Library, www.tricare.mil/afml
NN/LM Training and Educational Opportunities, nnlm.gov/training
NLM Classification, wwwcf.nlm.nih.gov/class
Medical Subject Headings (MeSH) Browser,
    www.nlm.nih.gov/mesh/MBrowser.html
The Basics of Medical Subject Headings, NLM,
    www.nlm.nih.gov/bsd/disted/mesh
Branching Out: The MeSH Vocabulary, NLM,
    www.nlm.nih.gov/bsd/disted/video
Using CINAHL Headings, Duke University Medical Center
    Library, www.mclibrary.duke.edu/training/cinahlheadings
Searching CINAHL With Subject Headings, McGoogan Library of
    Medicine, University of Nebraska Medical Center,
    app1.unmc.edu/mcgoogan/guides/CINAHLHeadings.html
CINAHL Support Center, support.ebsco.com/cinahl
Deciphering Medspeak, MLA, www.mlanet.org/resources/
    medspeak
Medical Terminology Course, Des Moines University,
    www.dmu.edu/medterms
MedlinePlus, medlineplus.gov

Chapter 3: It's All About the People

Open-Ended Questions for Reference Interviews, Infopeople, infopeople.org/training/past/2004/reference/open-ended_questions.pdf

The Consumer Health Reference Interview and Ethical Issues, NN/LM, nnlm.gov/outreach/consumer/ethics.html

"I Don't Give Medical Advice; I Dispense Quality Health Information," Infopeople, infopeople.org/training/webcasts/webcast_data/242

Recommended Books for a Consumer Health Library, Healthnet, library.uchc.edu/departm/hnet/corelist.html

Consumer Health Magazines and Newsletters, Healthnet, library.uchc.edu/departm/hnet/nlist.html

Consumer Health Internet Resources, Healthnet, library.uchc.edu/departm/hnet/inters.html

Guidelines for Providing Medical Information to Consumers, Healthnet, library.uchc.edu/departm/hnet/guidelines.html

MedlinePlus, www.medlineplus.gov

MedlinePlus Interactive Tour, www.nlm.nih.gov/medlineplus/tour/medlineplustour.html

Consumer Health Manual, NN/LM, nnlm.gov/outreach/consumer

The Librarians' Role in the Provision of Consumer Health and Patient Education, caphis.mlanet.org/chis/librarian.html

Consumer Health Information Specialization Program, www.mlanet.org/education/chc

Clinical Informatics Consult Service, Eskind Biomedical Library, Vanderbilt University Medical Center, www.mc.vanderbilt.edu/biolib/services/cics.html

Introduction to Evidence-Based Medicine, Duke University Medical Center Library and the Health Sciences Library at the University of North Carolina–Chapel Hill, www.hsl.unc.edu/Services/Tutorials/EBM

Evidence-Based Medicine Resources Tutorial, University of South
Carolina School of Medicine Library, uscm.med.sc.edu/
ebmtutorial

Supporting Clinical Care: An Institute in Evidence-Based Practice
for Medical Librarians, Dartmouth College,
www.dartmouth.edu/~biomed/institute2009

Expert Searching, MLA, www.mlanet.org/resources/expert_
search

PubMed Central, www.pubmedcentral.nih.gov

Don't Get Pinched Video, University of Texas Health Science
Center–San Antonio, www.library.uthscsa.edu/university/
nihpinch.cfm

Tutorials, Lister Hill Library of the Health Sciences, University of
Alabama at Birmingham, www.uab.edu/lister/faq/index.php?
askReferenceID=3&action=category&c=22

NIH Public Access Policy, National Institutes of Health Public
Access, publicaccess.nih.gov

American Medical Informatics Association, www.amia.org/inside

BioMedical Informatics Course Overview, courses.mbl.edu/mi

Medical Informatics Section, MLA, www.medinfo.mlanet.org

U.S. Department of Health and Human Services' Health
Information Privacy, www.hhs.gov/ocr/privacy

Library Success: A Best Practices Wiki, www.libsuccess.org

Chapter 4: Technology

Internet Professionals Society of Alabama, ipsaonline.org

Computer, How Stuff Works, computer.howstuffworks.com

EZproxy, www.oclc.org/ezproxy

EZproxy Database Specific Issues, Support, Training, and
Documentation, www.oclc.org/support/documentation/
ezproxy/db/default.htm

Meebo, www.meebo.com

Google Analytics, www.google.com/analytics

Ebling Library News, Ebling Library for the Health Sciences,
University of Wisconsin–Madison, ebling.library.wisc.edu/blog

Tour of the Health Science Center Library, University of Florida,
www.youtube.com/watch?v=Fg31F-9QJOk

University of Colorado–Denver Health Sciences Library Twitter
Page, twitter.com/UCDenverHSL

University of Buffalo Health Sciences Library Twitter Page,
twitter.com/UBHSL

University of North Carolina at Chapel Hill Health Sciences
Library Facebook Page, www.facebook.com/pages/Chapel-
Hill-NC/UNC-Health-Sciences-Library/10473632902#/pages/
Chapel-Hill-NC/UNC-Health-Sciences-Library/10473632902

AddThis, www.addthis.com

Duke University Medical Center Library Google Gadget Page,
www.gmodules.com/ig/creator?synd=open&nocache=1&url=
http://www.mclibrary.duke.edu/gadgets/mclgadget.xml&
nocache=1

Chattahoochee Technical College Library's Allied Health Bundle
on Delicious, delicious.com/nmtc_Librarian/bundle:Allied
Health

Chapter 5: Databases and Resources

PubMed, www.pubmed.gov

PubMed Online Training,
www.nlm.nih.gov/bsd/disted/pubmed.html

CINAHL Support Center, support.ebsco.com/cinahl

MD Consult, www.mdconsult.com

UpToDate, www.uptodate.com

NLM Mobile, www.nlm.nih.gov/mobile

PubMed for Handhelds, pubmedhh.nlm.nih.gov/nlm

AIDSinfo's PDA Tools, aidsinfo.nih.gov/PDATools/Default.aspx?
MenuItem=AIDSinfoTools

Handheld Computer Resources in the NCBI Bookshelf,
www.ncbi.nlm.nih.gov/entrez/query/Books.live/Help/mobile.
html

Mobipocket Reader, www.mobipocket.com/en/DownloadSoft/
DownLoadReaderStep1.asp

Radiation Event Medical Management,
remm.nlm.gov/Aboutthissite.htm#download

Wireless Information System for Emergency Responders,
wiser.nlm.nih.gov

Epocrates Rx, www.epocrates.com

Epocrates Product Feature Comparison,
www.epocrates.com/products/comparison_table.html

Diagnosaurus, books.mcgraw-hill.com/medical/diagnosaurus

Essential Evidence Plus, www.essentialevidenceplus.com

Skyscape, Inc., www.skyscape.com

Skyscape Free Products, www.skyscape.com/estore/store.aspx?
Category=35

PDA Websites, Florida State University College of Medicine,
med.fsu.edu/library/PDASoftware.asp

Cochrane Collaboration, www.cochrane.org

Cochrane Library, www.thecochranelibrary.com

Cochrane Library Help, www3.interscience.wiley.com/
cgi-bin/mrwhome/106568753/HELP_Cochrane.html

National Guideline Clearinghouse, www.guidelines.gov

TRIP Database, www.tripdatabase.com

Liberating the Literature, TRIP Database Blog,
blog.tripdatabase.com

National Organization for Rare Disorders, www.rarediseases.org

OncologySTAT, www.oncologystat.com

Health Sciences Online, www.hso.info

SportDiscus, www.sirc.ca/products/sportdiscus.cfm

ERIC, www.eric.ed.gov

EMBASE User Support, info.embase.com/user_support/
   learning_tools.shtml

Liblicense, www.library.yale.edu/~llicense

Chapter 6: Resources and Networking

MLA, www.mlanet.org

American Association of Colleges of Pharmacy—
   Libraries/Educational Resources Section, www.aacp.org/
   governance/SECTIONS/libraryeducationalresources/Pages/
   default.aspx

American Medical Informatics Association, www.amia.org

American Society for Information Science & Technology—
   Medical Informatics SIG, www.asis.org/SIG/med.html

Association of Academic Health Sciences Libraries,
   www.aahsl.org

Association of Mental Health Librarians, www.mhlib.org

Canadian Health Libraries Association, www.chla-absc.ca

Health and Science Communications Association, www.hesca.org

International Federation of Library Associations and
   Institutions—Health and Biosciences Libraries Section,
   www.ifla.org/VII/s28

Libraries in Medical Education SIG of the Association of
   American Medical Colleges' Groups on Educational Affairs,
   www.aahsl.org/mc/page.do?sitePageId=84885

NN/LM, nnlm.gov

Public Library Association, www.ala.org/ala/mgrps/divs/pla

Special Libraries Association (SLA)—Biomedical and Life
   Sciences Division, units.sla.org/division/dbio

SLA—Biomedical and Life Sciences Division, Medical Section,
   units.sla.org/division/dbio/medicalsection

Web 2.0 Resources, MLA, www.mlanet.org/resources/web20_
  resources.html

JMLA Case Studies in Health Sciences Librarianship, jmlacase
  studies.blogspot.com

NN/LM News and Announcements: Blogs, nnlm.gov/news

Bioinformatics @ Becker: Updates and Musings from the
  Bioinformatics Team at Becker Medical Library,
  beckerinfo.net/bioinformatics

Botsford Hospital Library Blog, www.botsford.org/library/blog

Dental Information & Library Innovation: News and Tips about
  Dentistry from the University of Michigan Dental
  Informationist (and friends), mblog.lib.umich.edu/dentlib

Maine Medical Center Library, mmclibrary.wordpress.com

Northern Virginia Community College Medical Education
  Campus Library, medicalcampuslibrary.blogspot.com

Spokane Public Library Health Blog,
  new.spokanelibrary.org/blog/health

davidrothman.net: Exploring Medical Librarianship and Web
  Geekery, davidrothman.net

Krafty Librarian, www.kraftylibrarian.com

Weblogs—Medical Librarianship, LIS Wiki,
  liswiki.org/wiki/Medlib_Blogs

NLM RSS Feeds for News, Podcasts, and Webcasts,
  www.nlm.nih.gov/listserv/rss_podcasts.html

MLA News RSS Feed,
  feeds.feedburner.com/MedicalLibraryAssociationNews

Ejournal Feeds by Topic, Ebling Library for the Health Sciences,
  University of Wisconsin–Madison, ebling.library.wisc.edu/rss

RSS4Lib: Innovating Ways Libraries Use RSS, www.rss4lib.com

*A History of the National Library of Medicine: The Nation's
  Treasury of Medical Knowledge*, www.nlm.nih.gov/hmd/
  manuscripts/miles/miles.html

NLM Email Lists, www.nlm.nih.gov/listserv/emaillists.html

NGC4Lib, dewey.library.nd.edu/mailing-lists/ngc4lib

SLA-DSOL, units.sla.org/division/dsol/Discussion.html

SYSLIB-L, listserv.indiana.edu/cgi-bin/wa-iub.exe?A0=SYSLIB-L

Web4Lib, lists.webjunction.org/web4lib

NN/LM Training & Educational Opportunities, nnlm.gov/training

National Training Center and Clearinghouse, nnlm.gov/ntcc

Educational Clearinghouse, nnlm.gov/ntcc/ch

Archived Webcasts & Webinars, Infopeople,
     www.infopeople.org/training/webcasts/list/archived

Kovacs Consulting, www.kovacs.com

Distance Learning Opportunities, MLA, www.mlanet.org/
     education/telecon

Academy of Health Information Professionals,
     www.mlanet.org/academy

Professional Competencies for Health Sciences Librarians, MLA,
     www.mlanet.org/education/policy/executive_summary.
     html#B

Health Sciences Information Knowledge and Skills, MLA,
     www.mlanet.org/education/policy/knowledge.html

Glossary

AAHSL. Association of Academic Health Sciences Libraries

AAMC. Association of American Medical Colleges

AHEC. Area Health Education Center

AHIP. Academy of Health Information Professionals

Clerkship. Part of the medical school curriculum that takes place in the clinical setting.

Clinician. A physician in a hospital or clinical setting.

Consumer health. Term used for the health and medical information provided to patients and their families.

DOCLINE. National Library of Medicine's interlibrary loan system.

EBM. Evidence-based medicine

EMR. Electronic medical record

HIPAA. Health Insurance Portability and Accountability Act

Index Medicus. Subject and author index of articles published in medical journals.

Informatics. Use of computer applications and technology in health care delivery, education, and decision making.

JCAHO. Joint Commission on the Accreditation of Healthcare Organizations. Now known as the Joint Commission.

LiME. Libraries in Medical Education

Loansome Doc. System for ordering documents found in MEDLINE through PubMed and National Library of Medicine Gateway.

Magnet hospital. Status awarded by the American Nurses Credentialing Center to hospitals that meet specific criteria in nursing quality.

MEDLINE. Bibliographic database from the National Library of Medicine.

MeSH. Medical Subject Headings

MLA. Medical Library Association

NCBI. National Center for Biotechnology Information

NIH. National Institutes of Health

NLM. National Library of Medicine

NN/LM. National Network of Libraries of Medicine

PICO. Acronym to help organize a clinical question; stands for patient or problem, intervention, comparison, outcome.

Point of care. Term generally used with information resources that can be used directly at the patient's bedside.

PubMed. Free online database that provides access to MEDLINE.

Resident. Medical school graduate who practices medicine under the supervision of attending physicians.

Systematic review. Literature review that seeks to answer one specific clinical question.

Woods Hole. Nickname for the weeklong biomedical informatics course held at the Marine Biological Laboratory in Woods Hole, Massachusetts.

About the Authors

Lisa A. Ennis

In 1994, I accidentally got my first library job. I was adjuncting in the history department at Georgia College. Since adjunct positions didn't come with benefits, I was on the prowl for something that would both allow me to keep teaching and give me health insurance. I didn't actually apply for a library job at all, but someone in human resources sent my application to the library. Much to my surprise, I was invited to interview for an interlibrary loan assistant position—and I was even more surprised when I was offered the job. I figured this was a perfect situation. I'd get to teach history and learn the ins and outs of the library while I decided how and where I wanted to pursue my PhD in history. The weird thing was, the more I learned about the library, the more I liked it. The more I thought about that history PhD, the less appealing it became. It wasn't long before the librarians picked up on this and began to encourage me to go to library school.

I succumbed to the pressure and entered the University of Tennessee's School of Information Sciences with every intention of being a systems librarian in an academic library. I graduated in 1997 and began the search for that elusive position. My first three years out of library school were spent trying to settle in and experimenting with an IT position in a mental health center. I loved the IT work but sorely missed the library environment so began to keep an eye open for library positions. One day while perusing the job ads, I noticed an advertisement for a reference and instruction librarian back at Georgia College. It wasn't systems, but I knew I would get to do techie stuff there, and I really wanted to be back in a library. As part of the interview I had to do a presentation and decided my topic would be athletic training resources. Apparently I did a good enough job, because I was offered the position. They also asked if, since I did such a good job on the presentation, I would be interested in having the School of Health Sciences as my liaison area. I happily agreed.

Then, when a reference position opened at Lister Hill Library of the Health Sciences at the University of Alabama at Birmingham, I decided I was ready for a change and applied. After only about a year in that position, the systems person resigned. I said I'd love to take that on, and they let me! Now I'm a systems librarian at a health sciences library, and I love every minute of it.

Nicole Mitchell

I attended Georgia College & State University (GC&SU) in Milledgeville, Georgia, home to what used to be the world's largest mental institution, author Flannery O'Connor, and Georgia's ante-bellum capital. Because I'd wanted to be a teacher since I could remember (I forced all my cousins to be "students" and used an empty wall in my grandparents' house for a chalkboard—how was I to know the ink wouldn't erase?), I decided I wanted to teach high school history. I enrolled in an education course with a practicum component to prepare me for the master of arts in teaching program. I had been a substitute teacher a few times, so I thought I would be fine. The day I stepped foot into that seventh-grade classroom was the day I knew that I was definitely not cut out to be a teacher. I didn't know what to do with a history degree at that point, but luckily for me, I was offered a graduate assistantship to pursue my MA in history. After I earned my MA, my mother tried to convince me that I'd be a good librarian, but that was the farthest thing from my mind.

So I applied for the job of assistant archivist for special collections at GC&SU's Ina Dillard Russell Library. To my surprise I got the job and found that I loved working in the library. But I wanted to do more. I thought about going to library school but wasn't sure where, since Georgia didn't have an accredited program at the time. I looked into a couple of distance education programs but finally decided to go to the School of Library and Information Studies at the University of Alabama. Beginning in fall 2005, I was excited to receive one of 10 Institute of Museum and Library Services' Academic Research Library fellowships designed to prepare students for careers in academic libraries. In addition to coursework, I got the chance to conduct original research projects—one of mine was on the graying of the profession.

It seems that I was destined to work in the health care arena. I worked throughout high school and college for a home health agency and even did some medical transcription for a while. I received my MLIS in December 2006 and joined Lister Hill Library of the Health Sciences at the University of Alabama at Birmingham as a reference librarian and liaison to the School of Optometry in January 2007.

Index

W

Walton, Linda, 137
Web 2.0 technology, 93–95, 97–98
Web4Lib (list), 142
web content, creating, 92–93
web servers, 87, 99
websites, library, 16
Wiki, Library Success, 70, 73
Wireless Information System for
    Emergency Responders
    (WISER), 115
Wisconsin—Madison, Ebling
    Library for the Health
    Sciences, University of, 93

Wood, M. Sandra, 136, 137
work settings, health sciences
    library, 1–2, 4–9

Y

YouTube resources, 93, 94

Z

Zoological Society of San Diego
    library, 12

More Great Books from Information Today, Inc.

The Accidental Librarian

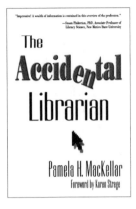

By Pamela H. Mackellar

Are you doing the job of a librarian without the advantage of a library degree or professional experience? Do you wonder what you might have missed in formal LIS education, how highly trained librarians stay on top of their game, or what skills and qualities library directors look for? Pamela H. Mackellar covers library principles, practices, and tools of the trade. She offers tips, examples, and simple exercises to increase your understanding. Whether you are seeking a thorough grounding in library fundamentals or looking for ways to serve more effectively in your current role, *The Accidental Librarian* is a great place to start.

432 pp/softbound/ISBN 978-1-57387-338-3 $29.50

The Accidental Library Marketer

By Kathy Dempsey

The Accidental Library Marketer fills a need for library professionals and paraprofessionals who find themselves in an awkward position: They need to promote their libraries and services in the age of the internet, but they've never been taught how to do it effectively. This results-oriented A-to-Z guide by Kathy Dempsey reveals the missing link between the everyday promotion librarians actually do and the "real marketing" that's guaranteed to assure funding, excite users, and build stronger community relationships. Combining real-life examples, expert advice, and checklists in a reader-friendly style, this is the complete how-to resource for successful library marketing and promotion.

312 pp/softbound/ISBN 978-1-57387-368-0 $29.50

The Accidental Technology Trainer
A Guide for Libraries

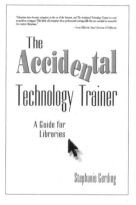

By Stephanie Gerding

Here is an extremely useful and reassuring guide for library staff who find themselves newly responsible for technology training. Stephanie Gerding addresses the most common concerns of new trainers, recommends great tools and techniques, and shares helpful advice from many of her fellow tech trainers. *The Accidental Technology Trainer* will help you get up-to-speed quickly and become a more confident and successful trainer.

272 pp/softbound/ISBN 978-1-57387-269-0 $29.50

The Accidental Fundraiser

By Julie M. Still

Many nonprofit, charitable, and other small organizations need funding yet cannot afford to employ a full-time fundraiser, relying instead on volunteers or staff members to raise the money. *The Accidental Fundraiser* is a practical guide covering all aspects of fundraising for the small organization, the volunteer, and the staff person in any setting who plans to take on a fundraising project for which he or she may not have been trained. Julie Still offers practical and reassuring advice that will help any individual become an effective fundraiser regardless of previous experience.

176 pp/softbound/ISBN 978-1-57387-263-8 $29.50